Wholistic Life Coaching

Washington

A Wholistic Life Coaching original

Text and cover © by Dr. K. Mhina Entrantt

All rights reserved. No part of this book may be used or reproduced in any manner whatsoever without permission, except in the case of brief quotations embodied in critical articles or reviews.

Published 2013

Printed by Lulu.com in the United States of America

Entrantt, K. Mhina

What Grandmother Knew about the

Law of Attraction and How She Taught Us: A Guide for people of colour

ISBN 978-0-9894793-0-1

Please call me by my true name so I can wake up, and so the door of my heart can be left open, the door of compassion.

THICH NHAT HAHN

*He who knows others is wise, but he who knows himself is enlightened.*

Lao Tzu

Awakening...

As I walked out my door,

Curiously wondering

what would be in store;

Walking towards my daily routine,

Admiring, the growth of my own self esteem.

Getting on the bus, looking for an empty seat;

I saw a whole family, pointing to a nearby one.

We smiled and nodded our heads,

I thought that would be the end.

Little did I know, it hadn't even begun.

Grandmother & Grandfather told me

how long they'd been riding this bus,

Just waiting for, this chance given to us.

I looked a lil puzzled trying to make sense of

What was said. Unable to grasp it,

I juss shook my head.

U
 N
  T
   I
    L

They told me they were the Ancient Ones, from My Tribe;

the Ones everyone thought had long ago died!

They told me how, they've been watching over me

Down through the years;

Rooting & Supporting, me in the Upper Atmosphere!

They Applauded my Progress and how I had never quit.

Through all the adversities/hard times/unexpected life kicks!

Momma died suddenly/daddy died later/bro got on drugs.

For quite some time in my life, seemed like

somebody was flipping all my rugs!

The hospital trips that seem like they would never end.

Love ones acting more like enemies than even distant friends!

Movin--movin==MOVIN--unsolicited==unwanted--moving!!!

Different jobs--different states--& certainly different pay rates.

aaaaaaaaaaaaaaaaaaaaaaaaaaaaaaaaaaaaaaaaaaaaaaaaaaaaaaa aaaaahhh!

I made it through!!!

The Chief Elder stood up--and every One hushed....

He said Daughter of My Ancient Line, Today is Your Day;

IT IS Your TIME!!

Not knowing whether to stand/bow, speak or retreat,

I just sat there heart pounding, glued to my seat!

He continued, to speak, the Journey for you has been rough, indeed.

And we are over joyed how you have overcame it all, and continue to succeed.

These events, that you thought were tragedies/travesties/calls for despair;

were actually your Elevation Tools, opportunities to learn what's

really important in Life and what should rule.

The Matriarche Herself Stood Up and the Chief Elder took his seat~

My Daughter of My Ancient Line, Stand up and Step Forward!

On Wobbly legs that would not stand, I reach back for a hand

and they gently pushed me up.

I bowed my head in Honor & Humility at the Glory of such a sight!

She held out her Scepter and 3 Aspirants jumped to their feet and

Gently, held my head up~

Mother Matriarche said You are the Scrybe-Vessele,

Broken Clay that has been Re-made!

You are Whole now, no need to be afraide,

let the past be buried w/ the dead~

As she said those words, I saw Thunder & Lightening Flashing

In the midst, of the glow of RA.

All I could do was stand in Awe!

I stood there unable to speak, as I felt something been wrapped around me...

It was a Cape that fell down to my feet, deep purple on the outside

and the reddest-of reds-on the inside.

Tears of emotions-upon-emotions, begin to fall from my eyes.

Mother Matriarche, came to My side and put something in My Hand

and closed my hand around it.

She Commanded all the others to close their eyes and bow their heads.

To me she said Look In Your Hand! THIS IS MY COMMAND!

I slowly opened my hand, not knowing, what I would see...

The Matriarche said, this is the Sacred Pen, made from the Baobob tree!

This will Heal the deepest of wounds,

Awaken those in the Great Slumber,

Soothe the Weary,

Help them break away from the tierany,

Inspire the Hopeless,

Encourage the Cast - Aways,

Be a Beacon from the Solar Rays.

I COMMAND YOU, TO NOW WRITE FROM THIS PEN!

I bowed and said YES...

When I rose my head,

the bus was empty!

and I was wearing my dress

I had on when I entered the bus.

I looked around in utter disbelief;

I felt tingling on the top of my feet

So I looked down, not knowing what to expect

Or what I would see...

To my surprise, when I fashioned my eyes

Down below

My toes were covered

In the finest of gold dust~

K. MHina Entrantt, © 2011

Why I Chose You

This is why I chose you,
my dear craftsman of the scribe.
I knew you could be trusted
and your words would never divide.
Maybe, separate the bound from prison,
maybe cause a dead soul to now be risen.
I knew you would hold your tool, the pen ever so sturdy.
I knew when it came to word-surgery,
you wouldn't mind getting dirty;
I had full confidence in your ability to be still;
that you wouldn't get caught up in some cheap, ego thrill.
I gave you, your tools, paper and pen;
Then I stood back, as I sent you among women and men.
I laughed at them when they laughed at you.
Thinking you were un-armed, what could pen and paper do?

You smiled at them in your own humble way.
They thought you were shy, didn't have much to say.

 But truth stands on its' own; Never asking others what is known.

I've sent you down in the valley, for great looks.
I've given you wisdom, beyond the greatest books.
I've sat you on the mountain tops, with no one else to speak.
I allowed you to live, where others are afraid to peak.
I've put words/syllables/signs/symbols on your lips.
I've even given your life, more than a few dips.

Wide is your journey and many you shall reach.
For I know what lies within you, that you were born to teach!

Down by the riverside you shall Drink Knowledge's cool waters, one handful at a time…

Just remain quiet and still, for the next word and line.

    K. Mhina Entrantt©2009

Guest Forward, Esther Jones-Alley

As I started to read the introduction of what had come from the mind of Mhina (Karen), I realized that I was truly blessed and fortunate enough to walk this sacred journey with her. I remember seeing and feeling the excitement along with her and I remember the exhaustion as Karen would complete yet another section of this story. I can recall having lengthy conversations with her after she had spent a long night with the ancestors as they directed her fingers across her keyboard. I remember the joy and surprise that she felt as she received wisdom from the ancient ones and how sometimes it was almost too much for her to articulate. But Karen held fast and put her whole heart and soul into birthing this baby. She truly displayed signs of a mother in labor, at times, as more and more unfolded within her.

The chapters on being home not just in a physical place but in all nine houses touched my soul and provoked me to go even deeper into knowing my own inner home. It was really timely for me since I was preparing to move back into my physical house after a long absence. I was in the process of repairing the physical structure and trying to be well in my soul with going back and syncing my energy with the energy of my house again. At the time, reading her words moved me far beyond the thought process I was engaged in, around going home. I felt supported as I knew that it would take **courage** to embark on such a huge project with so little resources to do the many repairs and not knowing where I would get them from. I knew that I would have to **trust** in the Universe to make a way out of no way so that my thoughts could be made manifest. It would take all of my **passion** to keep me going through the tough times and when it seemed the resources were short on this project. Armed with this information the task before me became easier and my appreciation for home grew deeper.

I gained a new understanding about prosperity when I read the section on money. I begin to see that money was not the goal. I had to be in the flow and accept however the resources and currency showed up. I got it—I really got it. It was as if a light went on in my head and I could see very clearly that currency had little to do with paper money and everything to do with abundance and the Law of Attraction. It hit me right between the eyes. What had been missing for me about the Law of Attraction was right here on these pages. It truly helped me to sort out my emotions around money and my relationship to it and how I used it. My association with money, prosperity and abundance will never be the same.

As I sat and held the completed work in my hands, I remembered each chapter as the words took form and through the pictures that appeared in my mind, as each story came alive. Mhina (Karen) seemed to bring together ancient Egyptian knowledge and modern day wisdom in a seamless flow of evidence that tells us we are all capable of much more than we have demonstrated thus far in our lives. She doesn't just tell stories, present information and share poems in this book, she gives specific instructions and inner active exercises to help you know yourself better and grow from that knowledge. By showing you how the farmer had to understand the cycles and rhythms of life, to plant and harvest his crops. And the way that plants and animal also adhere to cycles/rhythms she illustrates how one should be aligned with their own inner cycles/rhythms to live their soul's purpose. She pulls you into this world of animal medicine and natural remedies to help bring you closer to your roots, back to Mother Earth. She guides you through the streets of your past and pushes you onward to challenge yourself to have a better future.

This book is a tapestry of work woven together and interlocking like a jigsaw puzzle; made up of poems, short stories and proverbs. It is filled with perception, knowledge, and wisdom that has been imparted to her, by her many ancestors over a lifetime. Each event she experienced represents a piece of the puzzle, each poem she wrote represents another piece and each memory she wrote about also represents a piece of the puzzle and this book symbolizes how each piece connected together. By reading this book, you will see the completed picture that has been created through this sacred journey of this amazing scribe and historical storyteller. AMAZING I SIMPLY LOVED IT.

Esther Jones-Alley,
Spiritual Life Coach

Esther Alley, CPC
Spiritual Lifestyle Coach
Kent, WA
Phone: 206-355-0306
E-mail: aesther2@gmail.com
Website: www.Estherjones-alley.com
http://facebook.com/EstherJones-Alley

Coaching is a vehicle that moves you along life's journey. My primary focus is coaching individuals looking to live more authentically in all areas of their lives. Throughout my professional career spanning politics, local government, non - profit management, and entrepreneurship, I innately counseled and encouraged many individuals on issues as varied as corporate politics, job dissatisfaction, family issues, parenting teens, lost love, challenging toddler behavior, finding their spiritual connection, and career changes. At the time, I did not identify what I was doing as coaching. Today, I realize I have been coaching for a long time, way before I received the formal training and certification as a Coach. I use both Divine wisdom and Practical applications to help my clients co-create the most authentic life possible. My clients describe this co-creative partnership as deeply meaningful and life-changing! I continue to be enlisted as a Coach.

In allowing myself to be guided by intuitive logic and vision, I am able to support and assist my clientele and colleagues through challenging situations, career and personal transitions. With finely tuned sensibilities I encourage my clients to go deeper within themselves for answers to their pressing issues. I also support my clientele with a weekly video through my YouTube channel call Wednesday Wisdoms which are little tips, called Esther-isms. I also write and perform poetry and will be publishing my first book early 2014. My poetry comes from a place of inspiration deep within my soul. I draw from events and situation that occur in my life. My writing is not at will but is given to me spontaneously from my higher self.

Guest Forward, Irene Tcruz Shimizu

My husband and I met Dr. K when she was performing at a poetry reading one evening at a local theatre. I heard the passion and conviction of her words in her poem, "Work It Out and Stay." I sat up and took notice of this dynamic woman, and her words spoke volumes. She had the audience riveted, and at that moment I knew that I had found a new favorite author.

Dr. K is a gifted and insightful storyteller who weaves her magic with her life stories of ancestral wisdom, spiritual connection, and love. *What Grandmother Knew About the Law of Attraction and how she taught us* awakened many forgotten truths and memories that brought me back home. I read these words and I was transported to a time in my childhood when life was simpler, neighbors knew each other by name/family connections and exactly which kids belonged to what family. These stories brought back many memories of my long gone grandparents and my favorite godmother. They loved me unconditionally, and they took the time to pass on life lessons that I still remember today, and lessons that I am now passing onto my son.

I hear my grandmother's voice and can see her strong nimble fingers as she taught me to sew a button (and how to reinforce it) and what it meant to create a wonderful home life for the ones you love. I recall my grandfather tending his small vegetable garden in sunny San Diego showing me how and when to pick the leafy vegetables that taste the best in Filipino soups; and how to pray and give gratitude every night at sunset for your blessings. I can still feel the love when my godmother smiled and her eyes crinkled when her hands cupped my face and she fondly said: "You little stinker," which was followed by the best hugs. We are who we are because of our ancestral elders. I know that my ancestors went before me, but they are really still with me. Thank you, Dr. K for reminding me of this!

One of my favorite parts of this book is the call out that in nature there is a time and a season for everything. And so it goes for life's ebbs and flows. As we pass through our own seasons in our lives, the stories and the lessons in this book can help navigate the road ahead. Or give you pause just to enjoy the Now, and breathe into the moments of today.

And finally, I found myself gravitating towards the chapter on "The Ancient Rituals of Loving" and our lost Language. Find out what it means to be in alignment with ourselves and others. Only then will we have that balance and remember who we truly are.

Weaving history, science, poetry and life stories will delight the reader as they explore this fantastic voyage. Enjoy your journey!

Irene Tcruz Shimizu
Owner, Gabriel's Message
Irene@gabrielsmessage.com
206.419.8709

"I Truly Love What I Do"

Ever since I can remember, I have always loved paper…all kinds of paper. I followed my heart and while keeping my "day job" in 2006, I started my own paper arts company: GABRIEL'S MESSAGE.

My company is named after my son Gabriel and the Archangel Gabriel. I firmly believe that Life is about following your heart and your passion. And I have a passion for paper. Using Japanese Chiyogami papers I craft beautiful and colorful cards, journals, magnets, framed art, and other fun creations to make the spirit smile. With each creation I tuck in a little love, hope, and blessings for a wonderful life.

Author Forward

The idea that life lessons and spiritual principles, can be hidden in between the lines of a good story, a family phrase, or tradition doesn't seem unbelievable to me at all. Most people can tell you about at least one person in their immediate family or close circle, who is a great story-teller and the hearers of the stories are not always sure whether these stories actually happened or not, but the stories always leave an impression upon the hearer. These stories evoke deep emotions like belly laughter, contemplation, respect for rituals and living a balanced life. It is as though there are stories within the stories…if the hearer has the eyes to see and the heart to receive.

In the Ancient of Days, the Story-teller, Sage, Seer was a highly respected person in the community. They lived in or nearby the palace. They had the audience and ear of Pharoahs, Queens, Emperors, and Royal Advisors; as well as the people at large. Their position was sacred.

Our Ancestral Elders lived in harmony and alignment with nature, flowed with movement of the celestials, and honored all forms of life through the words of the

Great Storytellers. This rhythm was their way of life for as long as they honored the sacred words of the storytellers.

As kingdoms fell, ceded, or were captured, the visibility of the storyteller became less and less. Behind secret doors, the stories were still told, but only to a select few, who could be trusted with the sacred stories. As time went on, the words and ways of the storytellers were no longer honored or sought after and oral traditions faded into the walls, rocks, and hidden caverns. We lost touch with the messages and principles which were once given to society by the Great Storytellers. So now, we storytellers of the Way, are hidden in plain sight and only those with the willingness of heart and hunger of spirit can hear the voice of the sacred. Behind every story, are codes of behavior, spiritual principles, warnings, decrees, instructions and examples for the community. There are also global principles for all.

I set before you the sacred words of a modern day storyteller, may your heart be opened to what has been given unto you by divine decree and order. I chose to open a door, through short stories and poems about how my Grandmother taught our family about deep mysteries in a simplistic way.

As you read these stories, you will re-member your own observations and experiences with those who taught you about standards and principles of life, how to get through the twists and turns. Memories that have been buried for years, maybe decades will begin to reappear with deeper insight, wisdom, and messages. Some memories hold painful, confusing details, yet they too have their place in the tapestry of your life. The strong perspectives and absolutes of yester-years will now become available for review, release of trapped emotions, forgiveness, mercy, compassion and moving forward.

May a spark of new life, ideas, and truth unveil their way unto you. May the restoration of peace be your abiding companion, should you need it. May the pieces of your life puzzle begin to fit in place, and clarity become, your lotus blossom.

Dr. K. Mhina Entrantt,

A Divine Storyteller

Birthing This Book: Ancestral Gratitude!

I, Humbly bow in gratitude and awe to All of my Ancestors, who came forth to guide me through the labyrinth of writing and birthing this book! It is unlike anything I have ever written before! I am forever changed by the process that brought forth such an unveiling of the deep mysteries and the simplicities of life, which make up the Law of Attraction.

I am truly grateful to my paternal Grandmother, Mamie Keys, who guided me all along the way. I could feel her presence each time I sat down to my laptop to write another story. I also felt the guiding hands of others, such as my Maternal Grandfather, William Thomas, as well as the Ancient Ones further back in my Ancestral Line who presented the knowledge and understanding of the ancient ways. Also, I have never in my lifetime felt so Loved and Supported!

The writing of this book transformed me in Every aspect of my life, as deeply as the ancient serpents of the temples, when they would shed their skin and leave it behind, as they moved to another area within the temple. I was shown how to bring forth the Unknown and Forgotten, that you and I may find our way back to the Great Mother and our Path of Purpose.

When I began this journey, it was <u>unfathomable</u> that the depth of such a book would come through me!!! With wobbly knees and uncertainty of heart I took <u>each step</u> as I was guided to do so. I had the title of the book, way before the full concept of the book was clear. I didn't understand it, but I knew that was the title. The book began in a very simplistic manner, until I began to write about <u>Whatever you do, do it with excellence.</u> I literally felt the shift in my physical body, as the words, memories, principles of the Law of Attraction and the Spirit of Excellence began to flow…

From that day forward writing this book became a roller coaster ride! I wrote all hours of the day and night, my sleeping pattern changed, my eating pattern changed, my perspective broadened and the ancient ancestral ways presented themselves to me. Sometimes on weekends I wrote for 10-12 hours straight and it felt like 1 Or 2 hours had gone by! At other times I was awakened out of a deep sleep in the wee hours of the morning. Sometimes a word or phrase would come to me and that would be all, until I sat down to my laptop and the flow would begin.

As I surrendered and went with the flow, I began to have, almost daily esoteric experiences that I still grapple to articulate the experiences and how it transformed both Me and the book! It literally felt as though I was living in two worlds—one seen and the other unseen! I was both Author and Reader. I allowed the process to take me where I needed to go. I stopped resisting, I silenced my analytical mind and the ego…I just went with the flow! In six months, I completed this book!

I found my voice in a much deeper, ancestral, primal, organic, invigorating, mystical manner; wherein both the Author and Every Reader may have the alchemy experience of gold dust on our toes~

After completing this book, I too can say as the Apostle Paul is believed to have said, …forgetting the things that are behind me, I press forward toward the mark and the prize of the high calling… In writing this book, stepping forward with passion, purpose, and integrity I have said YES to my Path and the Way, which lies ahead. I now know with certainty I AM surrounded, totally wrapped, and clothed in Love with the doors of the Law of Attraction always responding to my deepest desires and aspirations.

I NOW know I CAN Have, what I embrace, and know I am deserving of. Only my own Ancestral Feminine Line could have come to me with such patience, healing, inspiration, guidance, and joy.

For this and so much more I am grateful beyond words!

I Thank Esther Jones-Alley for supporting me through this process and never doubting my ability to bring the book to its completion! I am most grateful for her words in the forward and look forward to reading her upcoming books which will be out in 2014. Esther is a spiritual life coach with a depth of knowledge about actualizing personal prosperity, alchemy, abundance, and connecting to all the universal laws. Her Wednesday Wisdoms on youtube are so packed full of passion, knowledge wisdom! If you are ready and willing to work on your path to purpose and abundance, Esther is the Spiritual Life Coach to assist you to get to the next level of completion and success. She has a few openings left for new clients, you definitely want to take advantage of such an opportunity as quick as possible!

I am also grateful to Irene Tcruz Shimizu who took time out of her busy schedule to read the manuscript and write a forward…Irene is an awesome artist who makes journals with Asian themes and other artistic expressions.…her products are nothing short of awesome;

not only are they beautiful works of art, there's a certain feeling of appreciation when you can have personal contact with the person who is creating your journal from scratch. I highly suggest that you support this wonderful Seattle artist.

I thank Chalice Stallworth for listening to my ideas at the very beginning of this process, giving feedback and recommending one of the photos, which really depicted my grandmother and her sisters.

Lastly, I thank you, the Reader for your willingness to join me on the path of Reconnecting with the Great Mother. May your journey be as exhilarating for you, as it continues to unfold for me…

Dr. K, Mhina Entrantt

Introduction

When I was a young child my elderly godparents used to babysit me while my parents worked. My godfather had a saying when I was doing something irony. He used to say: "you better stop before you get yourself into a hornet's nest." Those words would stop me in my tracks every time! He was soft spoken, somewhat frail, 90 year old man with skin the smooth color of dark chocolate and always had a smile, yet those words were more powerful than a person yelling STOP! My young mind could capture the visual his words painted. The symbolism of his words, were crystal clear.

I knew he was not talking about a literal hornet's nest, yet I understood, to be in a (figurative) hornet's nest, was not a good thing or an experience I wanted to have. Sometimes I didn't heed the warning and my Godmother would walk through the room while I was being irony. She would put me in her version of time out, which usually meant I had to sit on the couch for a "long" time or even worse I had to take a nap! Either way, before I left the room my godfather would say: "I told you, you were going to get in a hornet's nest." He said it in the same quiet voice he had given the warning.

At a young age I became intrigued with symbolic words, their meanings and the vivid pictures portrayed by them. I'm sure this became the fertile soil for the author/poet who would bloom many decades later.

During my coming up years, besides my mother there were 6 women who influenced my life by the way they lived theirs. These women defined womanhood for me:

My Maternal Aunts: Az, Lillian, Vivian

My Paternal Aunt: Eloise

My Godmother: Babe

My Paternal Grandmother: Mamie

I watched these women live their lives in a myriad of ways. Each was *very* different from the other. Each had their own way of being and presenting themselves, interacting with men, and determining how they would deal with main stream society. Two of my maternal aunts were nurses, one worked in a large mental hospital until she retired, while the other did private duty for the retired wealthy.

Some had formal education, some did not. Some had children, some did not. Some of these women were feisty, no nonsense, warriors, who could handle opposition of any kind with tenacity and verbal or physical responses as needed. Others seem to face the world, in a more softer, tone and manner.

Some were born in the late 1800s or early 1900s; while others were born right before/after The Great Depression.

It was a different time in the late 50's and 60's, when I was a child; there weren't sit-down discussions, fire-side-chats, or poignant stories while they tucked me in bed; I learned by watching how they dealt with life and how life dealt with them. It was the time before talk shows and reality TV. I can actually remember when we got our first console TV in 1962.

It had a black and white picture, we had about 10 channels and you had to manually turn the dial to change the channel! It had a prominent place in the living room and it remained the *only TV* for years. This was a time when all the closets were full-to-the-brim of things which were never discussed. The ways of becoming a woman was definitely at the top of the list!

It has taken 5 decades for me to capture the wisdom of what I learned from watching how these women lived their lives, especially during a time when women were financially dependent on men, not encouraged to have a voice about anything other than the comfort of others. The principles they shared with my immature, judgmental, naïve eyes are beginning to surface with clarity. The most clear at this time are the ones I "inherited" from my paternal grandmother. I've begun to realize I am in the grove with many other Hazelnut trees. My roots get deeper as I grasp the knowledge from the older, more mature trees.

There is a sacred Moorish principle, which describes the Hazelnut Trees as reminders to honor our ancestral mother. The Lessons of the Hazelnut trees teach us to give honor, learn from, and receive nurturance by connecting to our complete Feminine ancestral line. We are connected to the mother in body, mind, and spirit—even when we distance ourselves from the connection by our behavior and choices.

As trees in the grove stand one behind the other, so stand we, behind all the women on our father's side, joined with all the women on our mother's line. It is the tapestry of 23 chromosomes on one side and the joining of 23 chromosomes on the other.

On the physical, this is how a baby can come here looking just like his paternal grandmother or have eyes like his maternal great grandmother, who was long gone before the baby was born or have behavior, gestures, body type like those who have preceded him or her.

Hazelnuts are known world-wide for their nutritional value, full of protein, minerals, vitamin E, and antioxidants. Yet, no one can benefit from these things, until after the yearly harvesting time in Autumn—not early Autumn but towards the end. It is said, the best way to harvest the hazelnuts, is to *wait* for the leaves and nuts to drop, by themselves—no prodding, pulling, or snatching off too soon.

This is a significant Lesson of the Feminine Principle, of knowing when a cycle is completed and the time for release has come. There are rhythms, lessons, and messages all around us. Nature is waiting to teach us, if we open our hearts and eyes, knowledge and wisdom will flow unto us. The Great Mother teaches us how to respect the seasons, cycles and rhythms of life; to honor All life forms; to acknowledge the greatness of the plant, animal, minerals, stones, rocks, and crystal Kingdoms; to honor that All is in All.

 Sometimes our own leaves and nuts of experiences, understanding, or our willingness to change/ grow have not dropped from the trees of our comprehension level into the ripeness of maturity. It may be Autumn, meaning we are close to receiving the answers for our questions and solutions for our perceived problems; however it is not quite the end of the Autumn cycle *within us*, yet. There is still some ripening to take place, before we are ready for our leaves and nuts to drop of their own accord, signaling we are ready for the harvest and distribution of what we have learned in the hazelnut tree.

> *To Every thing there is a season, and a time to every purpose under the heaven.*
>
> *A time to be born, and a time to die; a time to plant, and a time to pluck up that which is planted…a time to break down; and a time to build up…*
>
> *A time to weep, and a time to laugh; a time to mourn, and a time to dance…*
>
> *A time to get, and a time to lose; a time to keep, and a time to cast away…*
>
> Ecclesiastes 3:1-2; 4, 6; King James Bible

 ## What is a Season?

The Ancient Ones determined a season by watching the animals, weather, sunlight, plant life and the celestials. Seasons are the result of the yearly revolution of the Earth around the Sun and the tilt of the Earth's axis as to the revolution. The tilt of the Earth on its axis allows the angle of the Sun to be higher in the summer and lower in the winter.

This titling of the Earth's axis is believed to be on a 30 degree angle, causing the southern and northern hemispheres to be in completely opposite seasons, always. The result is the changes in day light hours. The lower angle of the sun, during the winter, attributes to less direct and intensity of solar energy and the higher angle allows more direct light and intensity.

What is Rhythm?

Rhythm occurs when there is a pattern of movement, a frequency of strong, accented periods and low resting periods; timed movement or expression…

Music, Poetry, Language and Geometry are all said to have Rhythm. All of the voluntary and involuntary functions of the body have their individual rhythm and a collective rhythm. The heart beats in a certain pattern, elimination systems break down food and send it where it needs to go in a certain pattern of movement. The increase or decrease of sunlight impacts the rhythm of the entire body. We are constantly surrounded by Rhythms—syncopated, insidious, and effectual.

Plant life rhythm is what allows a plant to identify the season and know how to respond accordingly. Activity such as growth, germination, photosynthesis, and fragrance release are all a part of the rhythm of plant life. The plant aligns with the cycle of sun light of its environment. The intensity of the light allows the plant to know what to do next in their growth cycle. The plant is aware of the season, cycle, and rhythm and responds appropriately.

What is a Cycle?

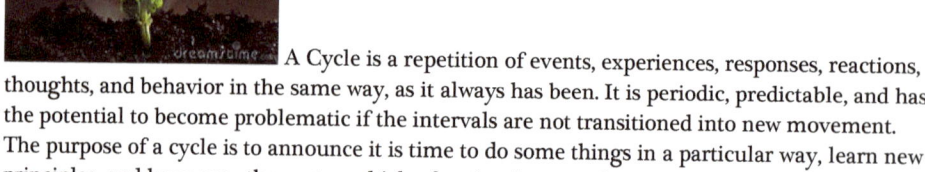

A Cycle is a repetition of events, experiences, responses, reactions, thoughts, and behavior in the same way, as it always has been. It is periodic, predictable, and has the potential to become problematic if the intervals are not transitioned into new movement. The purpose of a cycle is to announce it is time to do some things in a particular way, learn new principles, and have growth spurts—which often invoke great leaps of faith!

Since the beginning of days the Ancient Ones determined a cycle by the movement of the sun/stars. For example, a day was considered a cycle, as was a year—each centered around, the earth's rotation. The cycles of the moon was just as important to the Ancient Egyptians. They consistently observed the celestials and knew it usually took the moon a little less than 30 days for the moon to complete its phases and to go from one full moon to the next. They also knew every 18 years, the earth, sun, and moon were just about in the same position, which is what attributed to solar and lunar eclipses. Our Elders governed their lives by the cycles of all of nature. They studied their environments above and below and knew it well. They knew and lived in alignment without telescopes, computers, TV, or the internet, a world we still grapple to know and understand.

Although a cycle is circular in movement, it is meant to spin into the next level of growth, maturity, understanding, participation, activity and life itself. It is not meant to be a place of stagnation or destination…it is a pit stop. The journey is not over.

It is the assignment of the seed to grow at full capacity, *according to the cycle it is in.* All, of the seed's destiny, is already within the seed, when it is dropped in the ground! Yes it will need the right soil, nourishment, sun light, and water to complete the full cycle; however All of what it is to become, lies within the seed. The acorn is the great oak tree and the oak tree is the acorn, for they are inseparable.

Just as the rings of the trees show its development, so are the cycles of development for a young girl until she reaches her bloom of development as a woman. When a girl begins her menses she has biologically stepped on the *path* of going towards womanhood. During the ancient times there were women in the community who could explain to the girl what this meant literally, symbolically, and spiritually. She was taught about the energy of the moon and the sacredness of feminine principle. She was taught to read the stars, know their positions and how the celestials influenced all of nature. She was guided through her stages of development and she was present when the women of her kin told their stories about womanhood—stories that reached back to the ancestral mother.

It is the same principle for a young boy to capture the understanding of the yin and yang within and without. When he is shown the lessons of nature and how every life form is important to his world; how the ebb and flow of life can show him how to be balanced in body, mind, and spirit—it gives him the map he can refer back to over and over again in adulthood.

It takes determination, strength, and courage for the seed to gain what it needs in the darkness and continue to grow, until it is time to push through the dirt—to rise to the beckoning of the sun, to come forth into the next cycle. The internal clock tells the seed when it is time to go to the next cycle, it signals the alarm for the next stage of growth and the seed responds.

We have so disconnected ourselves from the internal divine messages of ebb and flow, that our internal clock, rhythms, seasons, and cycles are muzzled by our beliefs, choices, and attachment to non-spiritual gratifications. Hue-mans have forgotten how to begin their day with gratitude, expectation of good, preparation for good, and willingness to be taught by the lessons for that day. Hue-mans have lost touch with closing their day in gratitude for completion of the day and wisdom gained.

Our lack of insight and poor judgment, often lead us into downward spirals and cycles because we misinterpret certain events in our lives—we become sad, hurt, bitter, confused, angry and we give up; instead of pressing forward.

When the exact same cycle is allowed to repeat itself, dominate, and control; the cycle has become an abnormal pattern of repetition. It has been allowed to go beyond its divine intent and purpose. K. Mhina Entrantt

It is a natural progression for a seed *to live and grow in darkness for part of its growth cycle. All darkness is not a sign of death—it may actually be a sign of individual incubation or a cocoon period; a setting aside for deep internal growth.* There are times when a person must be willing to go within their own darkness and do the inventory on what beliefs, opinions, and past actions are useful and will stay and which ones have <u>outlived</u> their usefulness and must go. The darkness is not a scary place, there are no boogey men—only growth waiting for you to step into your next cycle.

The ways of the Great Mother have been systematically removed from group consciousness and frightened, willful, un-mothered children have been left in charge of the house. The outcome has not been good. The Feminine Principle awaits the return of her worn and weary children.

In all of nature there is an ebb and flow—seed time, harvest time. It is not winter for the entire year. There is a natural flow into the next Season, Cycle, or Rhythm. The birds know when to migrate, the salmon know when to make their voyage, bears know when to hibernate, and trees know when to release their leaves. It is only hue-mans who ignore, minimalize, and disconnect themselves from their internal seasons/cycles/rhythms. We often eat, rest, work, invent and relate to one another… off season or in the wrong cycle or out of our own timing and rhythms. We are all, out of alignment in some areas in our lives. It is the Great Mother who can bring us back to our senses…back to our know…ings…back home!

A Woman's Decree of Sovereignty!

She said: It is not the men I've loved…the children I've raised…

Nor the bills I've paid, that makes me who and what I AM Today.

It is not my degrees and certifications or my acceptance in

Professional associations that prove, I've made my mark.

Yet there IS an interweaving…a spinning in and out of phases—

Of growth…of new birth…of letting go…of walking away…of closing doors…of A-ha moments springing forth out of moments of confusion, chaos and challenges upon which each breath was labored!

In the midst of the spins, something deeper,

more precious,

absolutely irrevocable

begins to come forth from within.

I in turn begin to savor every step…

To cling to every thread of the tapestry…

I begin to realize, embrace and accept

within each threading were hidden pieces of me.

And for the first time in my life, I wept at the recognition of Me!

I continued going down my own path until I reached a place that what I thought hurt me the most, has given me the greatest gifts;

For I refused to allow the 3 horsemen—Resentment, Bitterness, and Unforgiveness to become life-long companions.

They often tried to slip in, when I was at my wits' end, but in the end I Always knew I would rise again! And I did!

Embarking upon this Journey has given me the courage to live my own Truth…

It has Given me the fierce Decision to be Me— To stand with Integrity, Self-Respect, and Self Love.

To Greet Others with the honor of my words and my deeds—that what I say matches what I do…

Most importantly the beaten, tattered, closed down heart that I tucked away looong ago has been transformed by the many expressions of Love, from within and without and

Today, I AM Free~

K. Mhhina Entrantt ©2013

Getting in the flow with the Master Internal Clock

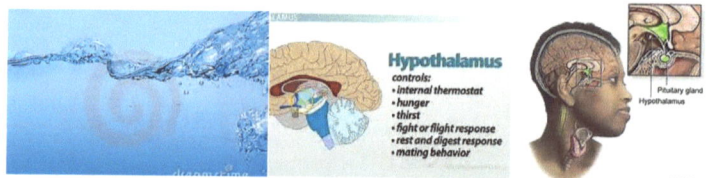

Getting in the flow with the Master Internal Clock

The natural rhythm, cycles, and seasons of hue-mans is located in the hypothalamus. There are groups of cells known as SCN (suprachiasmatic nucleus.) These cells receive messages about sun light from the eyes. In the eyes is the retina, which has photoreceptors, sometime referred to as rods or cones which allow vision. The retina also has ganglion cells that are photosensitive and project to the SCN.

This process activates our internal master clock—the *circadian rhythm clock*. This critical data regarding the time of the day/season/cycle that comes through the eyes, travels to the internal clock in the brain, which in turn allows the entire body to be in rhythm/in-synch/ aligned with the master internal clock. Each system and organ of the body has its own clock and all of the clocks must be in tuned with one another for the body to function appropriately. By the light that goes through the retina the body knows when to regulate body temperature; when to awake; when to sleep; when to eat; when to drink, etc. All the systems are *manned* by the internal master clock.

The use of the word *circadian* is associated with Franz Halberg from the late 1950s, to describe this process. This *circadian rhythm clock* resets itself daily by the 24-hour- rotation cycle of earth.

Chinese medical writings, which date back to the 14th and 13th century, described, what is now referred to as, *the circadian rhythm clock*. The writings went into great detail about the effect of the rotation on the sun on the body, as well as the effect of light. Two well-known writings of that period are-- Noon and Midnight Manual and the Mnemonic Rhyme to Aid in the Selection of Acu-points According to the Diurnal Cycle, the Day of the Month and the Season of the Year.

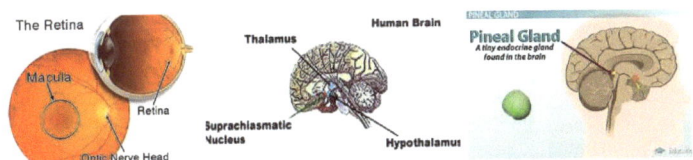

The internal "master clock" is dependent on the intensity of light going through the retina. The angle of the light carries the messages of what time it is, in terms of functioning of the body —is it time to get up or to go to sleep? Is it time to eat or release waste? Is it time to secrete hormones or not? All of the voluntary and involuntary systems of the body function and respond according to this process. The SCN takes the information of the lengths of the day and night from the retina, interprets it, and passes it on to the pineal gland, a tiny structure shaped like a pine cone which is located on the epithalamus.

 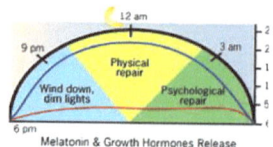

In response to the messages from the SCN, the pineal gland begins to secrete the hormone melatonin. Secretion of melatonin peaks at night and ebbs during the day and its presence provides information about night-length. Research shows the circadian rhythms impact the reticular activating system, which allows one's state of consciousness to remain intact.

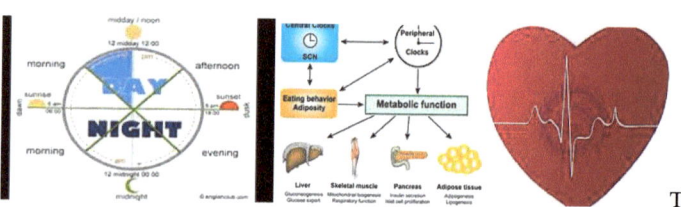

The various cells of the body are able to function and communicate with each other with precision, as a result of being in alignment with the master internal clock. There is a synchronized output of electrical signals going on through the various phases and cell activities—the whole body.

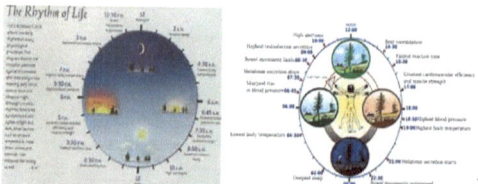

In the brain, the endocrine glands have staggered releases of hormones. This is an intricate process, which includes receptors throughout the body. The alignment and/or misalignment impact all the organs of the body. Any disruption, alignment issue, or out- of -cycle timing of the internal circadian rhythm clock, greatly impacts the body, mind, emotions and spirit of an individual.

According to a 2010 study by the Lighting Research Center, daylight has a direct effect on circadian rhythms as well as, on performance and well-being. Disrupting circadian light in the morning impacts the dim light melatonin onset by 6 minutes a day, for a total of 30 minutes for five days. The research showed that students who experience disruption in lighting schemes in the morning experienced disruption in their sleeping patterns. The change in their sleeping patterns had the potential to adversely affect their attention span and performance.

Individuals who work swing shifts or multiple shifts that cross multiple time zones regularly, such as frequent business travelers, airline personnel, and long distance truckers often have challenges with their circadian rhythm clock. Some challenges noted by researchers included: seasonal affective disorder (SAD) and delayed sleep phase syndrome (DSPS.)

It was also noted by researchers that persons in these occupations and similar ones, by the nature and times of the occupation, may have periods of out-of-synch eating patterns. These patterns may be a factor in altered insulin sensitivity, higher body mass, hypertension, inflammation, etc.

This research clearly shows it is not just what we eat, but when we eat. The physical body is built to be a well-oiled-machine with built-in cycles, rhythms, seasons. This is no different than our computers that will give us messages for updates or blocked viruses or the messages in our cars' dashboard. One can only ignore the flashing lights for so long before the engine fails, a hose bursts. As so, with our internal master clock, we are either in alignment or out of alignment and either state will manifest itself throughout every aspect of our lives~

The system is *programmed* to monitor itself and when we are in alignment with our internal master clock, the systems within and without, work at full capacity, as it was designed to do and we are in AT-ONE-MENT.

The modern world has been socialized and indoctrinated to be inundated, impressed by, and place all the value on left brain activity of logic and analysis. The world of rhythms and cycles, intuition and subtle instructions, ebb and flow—are readily dismissed, devalued, and rejected. In so doing, there are a lot of informed, data-filled, disconnected people, who are searching for something to fill the void that still lies within. That void is the lack of Feminine energy, lessons, and principled-stories in their lives. *There are no sustaining ideas, new birth, creation, transition, insight, wisdom, relationships without the ancestral mother.*

As the hazelnut trees are never alone in the grove, when they go through their cycles of growth, seasonal change, and expansion; neither are we. There are those who have gone before us, faced adversity, unexpected events, gave love, gave birth, buried the dead, faced seed time and harvest time in literal and symbolic ways and got through life on their own terms. There are many messages to be gained from the Hazelnut Trees, it begins with the *Honor* of being a woman, feeling connected to Mother Earth, tapping into your personal creativity and letting it flow; as well as meditation, prayer, and intuition. It is the place of transformations, balance, forgiveness of self and others…

 The Hazelnut Trees whisper on the gentle breeze and hope we will follow their lead to tap into the kinship mother, our genetic memory of nurturance, protection and transformation. There is a place for you in the Hazelnut tree grove even when your personal experience did not have a nurturing feminine presence in your life.

 If we look to Mother nature She can give us the answers we seek…there are natural rhythms to plant, grow, rest, hibernate, bloom, harvest, receive oxygen, air and sunlight. According to our elders there are certain activities that should take place during specific hours of the day.

 It is said every 2 hours, we are in a different nature activity stage and all of this is based on the *angle* of the sun at that time. The angle of the sun is very different at 6 AM than it is at 12 Noon or 6 PM. All of nature responds to the pull/push of the celestials. Plants don't open up at midnight to get sunlight, they align with the season/cycle/rhythm of their internal environment.

 We too must ask ourselves what is the angle of the sun in our lives, not the literal sun but the symbolic sun. From a personal perspective, we must know what time is it? We must know what cycle/season/rhythm we are in, in order to function at our full potential. Are you the one who works well with your hands and can fix anything? Or are you more suited to figure out math and science projects? Do you work well in a group or better on solo projects? Are you a leader? Or group participant? *We must KNOW ourselves in order to be true to ourselves!*

Nature shows us her examples, all the time. Bears hibernate throughout the winter and birth their young in the spring. This is a lesson about knowing when it is time to *sit* with the idea/dream/vision; nurture it, allow it to grow at its own speed and pace, and to protect it. It is imperative that we answer these questions with integrity and self- alignment: what are my peak inspiration times, when I am in the flow? What are my *off-peak* hours/days? How much sleep do I need to feel well-rested?

A good idea at an inappropriate time will die because it was not mature enough to withstand the transition at the next level. It is not that the idea wasn't good or didn't make sense or that it does not have great potential. *The problem is, the idea was out of season…out of cycle…out of rhythm.* Various fruits and vegetables grow at different times of the year, in different climates. We Must Wake Up and become Aware of Our own Seasons!

True signs of immaturity are: lack of patience, not being willing to wait for instructions, needed information, guidance, and not being aware of the signs of the season/cycle/rhythm of their own lives. Contrary to popular opinion there is not a race to win

43

and no reason for everyone to be running as fast as they can to out-do/out-shine/out-run…the perceived competitor. Yes there are occupations which have various levels and frequencies of intensity; and we must know ourselves well enough to be able to align the choice of work with our natural rhythms and inclinations.

 The- Super- Cape-Choice-of-Occupation, we had in our 20's and 30's may not be the right alignment for 40+. Or we may now decide to stay in the same field, but in a different capacity. We've lived some life, had experiences, and drawn some conclusions we did not have early on. What made your heart sing when you started your career, may have lost its harmony—only you know for sure, as you spend ample time with the feminine principle—The Great Mother.

It has been many moons since the Mother has been given the True Honor She is due. Are you tired, worn, weary …go to the hazel nut trees that you may receive compassion, support, refreshment for your body, mind, spirit.

NEWSFLASH: *Absolutely no one can do what you were born to do with the level of natural flow like you. All of nature…All of divine essence supports you, as you <u>align</u> with your birthright destiny~*

One of my favorite authors, Clarissa Pinkola Estes, in one of her books referred to a dream she had where she was standing on the shoulders of an old woman. When she tried to exchange places with the old woman she was not allowed to and she was told that was the way it should be. When she looked down she saw each old woman standing on the shoulder of an even older woman. I was fortunate enough to spend the first 5 years of my life in the presence of the Feminine Principle in full bloom, because my 80 year old Godmother was my daycare! Not only was she my grandmother's friend, she also had known both my parents since they were children. She knew the family stories—the good and the not so good. She nurtured me in a way that only a woman who had lived 8 decades could have. Although my tender eyes were too young to understand what I was truly experiencing, my spirit captured it and allowed it to lay dormant within for many years.

I remember as a child, if we showed *any* signs of catching a cold/flu, my mother would reach in the medicine cabinet for what I considered the worst-tasting medicine ever-Cod liver oil , *Three 6s, Castoria, or Father John's*. Each of these medicines had a component that "cleaned your system out." She and all the adult women I knew honored the wisdom of allowing the body to get rid of unwanted things. No matter what the ailment, their first line of attack was to clean you out—give you an enema or some herb that would flush your kidneys and your intestines.

They knew how to put warm oils on a cloth, rub the oil on your chest, back and arms and wrap you up while you rested in bed to "draw out the cold." They boiled fresh vegetables and had us "drink the broth" or what the ole folks called "pot liquor" while we were recovering. All the minerals, vitamins and seasoning were tastily blended together. It was warm so it felt good on sore throats and tight chests. It tasted good and it would remain when everything else was battling an upset stomach. All of these old remedies would lull you to sleep and you felt so much better the next day and you felt loved. These women did not talk about what the white blood cells were doing; how the immune system was being strengthened, or the benefits of dark leafy vegetables; they just did what needed to be done and the results were always 100%!

These women were "Naturopaths" practicing homeopathic care for the family way before it became popular or accepted by large portions of main stream society. We lived in the city, yet my mother always had a garden with peppermint, dandelion and a few other green sprouts, that were used to make teas. This was always a part of my world and I didn't question it. It was decades before I understood the significance.

When I was coming up, women in your tribe, kin, and close groups demonstrated to young girls like me how to navigate the world we lived in, how to navigate through the family system and how to have some deep part of your essence tucked away just for you and the divine. My young little eyes often thought the women were passive, powerless, and without options; because their words and actions were seldom done with a direct approach, putting their foot down, or setting the record straight. I had no idea what I was looking at!!! I am just beginning to get Clarity on the level of *Alchemy* these women demonstrated.

I recall once when jobs were scarce and layoffs were all around. I overheard one of my mother's friends tell her she did not have enough food to make dinner for her large family. My mother said I have a chicken, another one said she had vegetables, and my mom's friend said she had vegetables and could make lots of cornbread. These three women combined their resources, while the men were at work. The women agreed to use what they had and create a meal for all three families.

My mother brought the big pressure cooker pot along with the chicken, the other women gathered what they had too. Although I heard bits and pieces of the women's conversation, I was too young to really grasp the significance. I ran off to play with the other children. Those 3 women worked together seamlessly in my mother's friend's large kitchen. The aroma of the food cooking was wonderful!

These women manifested enough delicious food to feed over 20 people and have left overs! When the adults said grace over the food, I felt a deep feeling of gratitude and peace in the air. I was too young to fully understand what I was experiencing, but *I felt* it just the same. A sense of community, laughter, and great satisfaction filled the air. The men talked about men stuff, the women talked about women stuff and the children played and had a good time! When it was time to go, everyone hugged, wished each other well and had leftovers to take home.

This was one day in my normal and Today I AM Humble, Grateful, Wiser.

How to use this Book

This Book is about the simplicity of The Law of Attraction in the lives of everyday people. It guides the reader into the modern day world of storytellers, quests, alchemy, and everyday pots of gold, just waiting to be seen... This is a book of simplicity, stability, and symbolism. Everyday miracles are all around us and we often miss them, for we do not have the eyes and awareness to see, what is hidden behind the obvious. My Grandmother lived a very basic life, according to the view of my childhood eyes. I thought my generation was more in-tuned and ready for the world. I could not have been more wrong! The subtle lessons of my grandmother's generation have become as priceless jewels to me now. It has taken 5 decades to begin to grasp the depth of the life she lived!

In my lifetime, the world has changed 180 degrees and seemingly upside, down. Although I enjoy many of the new goods and services, technology, transportation and the like; there are many seemingly lost principles and standards, which I long to see again. I share this book with you that, *like may attract like.* The time has come for us to Return to our Mother, the feminine principles and energies upon which all creation is dependent upon.

Many of the aspects of our world, as we know it today has purposely, intentionally, and systematically removed the Mother from the equation. In so doing, we have lost our way...our manner...our nature. I present this book as one of the steps to make your way back Home.

This is a life-changing book, slow and easy is the way. May you feel the embrace of the Mother, on every page and may you respond in acceptance of the gifts given. It should be read slowly and more than once. It is not a book to be read straight through, for the messages, lessons, and symbolism are deeply stirring and require time to digest and incorporate what has been read. I suggest you read the book in small segments, that you may have time to adjust to the awareness, insight, and ancient wisdom this book awakens. I also suggest you keep a journal to record your memories, thoughts, journey, and awakenings. I use hand-made journals from a local vendor-artist, Irene Tcruz Shimizu, who wrote one of the forwards.

This is a life-changing book, slow and easy is the way. May you feel the embrace of the Mother, on every page and may you respond in acceptance of the gifts given.

The book is divided into three sections and each section has a theme and specific points for reflection, clarity, and insight.

Part I: The Making of a Matriarche

ClipartOf.com/61736 In the first section I introduce my paternal Grandmother, Mamie to you by describing her heritage and major challenges which influenced her life; such as the death of her first husband, life as a housekeeper, remarriage, relationship with her sisters and her life in the church world. I use these stories to give you the feel of life in the 2oth century for a woman of colour….

After the introduction to Grandmother and brief descriptions of her world, I give you 5 of the principles she used to teach us about life and the Law of Attraction. Each principle is represented by a tea cup, as beautiful teacups and saucers were permanent fixtures at her house. She always had a large box of tea and beautiful tea cups with matching saucers to serve tea in.

Part II: The 9 Aspects of Home

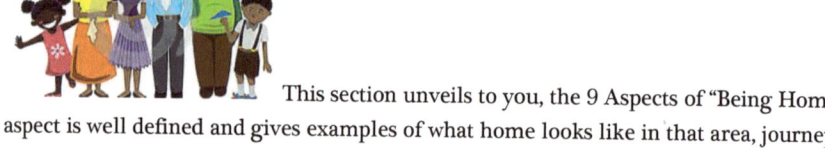 This section unveils to you, the 9 Aspects of "Being Home." Each aspect is well defined and gives examples of what home looks like in that area, journey obstacles, and ways to get home…

Part III: Coming Home This section begins with my first allegory. It is about the journey of going home. The section also gives the reader the opportunity to create and write their own allegory about their journey of getting home, journey obstacles, and decisions along the way.

Dedication

I dedicate this book to all the women who have crossed my path and left nuggets of wisdom for me to gather, ingest, and rely on when I needed it. The list of women pioneers in my life began with my mother, Ruth a woman wise beyond her years, extremely intelligent, and business savvy of the highest degree. A musician, vocalist, nurse, teacher and One who was passionate about giving back to the community! She departed this life at the young age of 43; however she left a field of wisdom for me to stumble upon time after time.

To my maternal aunts: Az, Lillian, and Vivian women who showed me the importance of being financially independent, having the courage to live and speak my own truth.

To my paternal aunt, Eloise who demonstrated the necessary principles of living a traditional life, how creative remodeling a home can be, and how to reinvent yourself, after the children are grown.

To my paternal grandmother, Mamie, who we always called "Grandmother" in a tone that exuded the same tone you would've used if you were referring to the Queen of England-formal respect and reverence. Decades have long passed since she left this plane, yet I am just starting to understand the depths of womanhood and principled footprints, she left for me to step on the path. My Grandmother and I truly came from different worlds. She was almost retirement age when I was born. She, a transplant from the Floridian-Georgia line, while me a city born New Jersey girl, of middle class parents who were the first to break the color line in their community in the late '50's. My normal was not fathomable for her, her entire life. Yet, we were kin by ancestral bloodline and behind her stood all the rest of my Feminine Ancestral line. They stood with all of their experiences, wisdom, insights, musings, strength and power. It has taken me over 5 decades to stumble across, bump into, and finally sit down in front of, this open door...

Finally, I dedicate this book to all those who will come behind my footsteps; those of the same ancestral line and those of other ancestral lines. The Feminine Principles of life await us all and will respond to our slightest invitation...

May the path paved through this Scribe inspire you to live a more authentic life, to reach for your deepest dreams and passions, to honor yourself and others with integrity, to step upon your path in joy and anticipation of daily miracles. This is my Intent and Decree.

K. Mhina Entrantt Winter, 2013

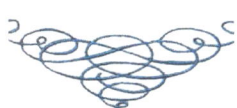

"This is a book that should be in every home in America! The depth and inspiration of the book left me speechless!" Mary J. Seattle Washington

"I cannot remember when I've read such a moving piece. It made me recall memories and dreams I had long forgotten. I am forever changed by reading this book." Gary W. Detroit Michigan

"I'm buying copies to send to all my sisters and brothers so we can keep the lively stories and lives of our grannies alive." Kerry C. Wichita, Kansas

"I generally read educational and academics, but the title of the book caught my attention. It was the best book I've ever read! It really made me look at everything in a different perspective. Sandra C. New York

"My favorite part of the book was the section on money. I've read a lot of books in lots of genres and I had never seen money explained in such a profound way." Keith S. Dover Delaware

"I could not put the book down, it left me on the edge of my seat. The more I read, the more I wanted to read. It was so good, I had to read it a second time." Beverly T. Los Angeles, California

"I recently loss my grandmother and was quite tearful when I saw the title of this book. As I read it my tears of sorrow begin to change into tears of joy, remembering my grandmother's house and her little sayings. This book brought me wisdom and comfort. Thank you." Sadie M. Atlanta, Georgia

Part I: The Making of A Matriarche!

My Grandmother was a Proud, Coal-Black-Woman, nearly 5' 10" tall, medium build, a Floridian by birth and descendent of the Moors. She had very little education, yet she was one of the most industrious women of my childhood. She did "Day's Work" which meant she was a housekeeper for various rich families in the surrounding area. Her own house was ALWAYS immaculate, with impeccable taste, as the saying goes, you could eat off her floor! Grandmother became a widow in the early 1930's raising 3 children on her own-2 boys and a girl. Her husband died of Pneumonia, because he could not get treatment at the white hospital and died on the way to the "colored" hospital. At the height of the Depression she had to find a way to feed and shelter 3 children. The children were 3, 5, and 8 years old. After her husband died, she moved from a country town to the city. It was closer to her family and friends in the church. Neither she nor her children really talked about their growing up years, but it doesn't take much insight to know those were hard times for this single mother. Somehow, she and her children made it through. The boys grew up, went in the military and eventually married. The daughter also married and created a beautiful home of her own.

I remember Grandmother's house was full of beautiful doilies on the arms of her cushioned chairs and couch, crystal candy dishes, decorative lamps of all shapes and sizes, oriental rugs on the living-room and dining-room floors. The doilies were small or tall ones which looked like miniature ruffle dresses without the top half, they sat regally on coffee tables, end tables and sometimes as the centerpiece. The deal was they were dipped in liquid starch and ironed. That's what made them stand up.

In the church world she was the District Florist for all the church events. The flowers were artificial, yet the arrangements she created were breath taking. She made them look as though they were fresh flowers—she was self-taught. She was devoted to her faith in God and the auxiliaries in the church. From her pill box hats to her white gloves, fancy coats, and pulled back bun she demonstrated an independent woman at a time where my eyes were too young to capture what I was seeing. We did not have fireside chats or milk and cookies at the table, yet as an adult I am able to capture the wisdom of her footsteps.

There were only a few family stories regarding my grandmother. There were 2 that I never forgot, one I overheard the adults talking about it and the other Grandmother told me herself…

The new husband: on the advice of a close church friend and church officials Grandmother married a widow minister who had moved to the area and joined her church. It was somewhat of a church-arranged marriage for the widow and the widower. Since Grandmother already had an established house with her children, it was decided that the new couple would reside in her home.

Within a few months of the marriage, my Grandmother learned her new husband was mean and cruel to her and her children. She sought the guidance of her church leaders, as divorce was unacceptable in her faith, as well as society at that time. At the meetings her husband would promise to mend his ways and be kind to his new wife and step-children, apparently just to please the church officials. Once he went back home he remained mean and cruel.

One evening there was a disagreement and the new husband attempted to hit Grandmother, but he missed because she was quick and strong. That night Grandmother packed his belongings and called the church officials to come pick him up, for she was done! This was UN-HEARD-OF, for women of that era! Although the new husband pleaded and tried to reconcile with Grandmother for quite some time, including soliciting the help of the church officials and her close friends to get back in her good graces. Grandmother never reconciled. She went back to the last name of her beloved first husband and never married again.

The Stolen Money: Grandmother had a saying, that you should always have a good coat and a nice pair of shoes on when going out into the public. She said it kept outsiders from being able to determine your status by the way you looked. She kept this rule even when she was going to clean someone's home. Her habit was when she arrived at the house she was going to clean, she always hung up her coat and purse in the closet by the front door and then she began to do her work for the next few hours. At the end of her time, when the job was completed, usually the woman of the house would pay her in cash for her services. On this particular day, things seemed to go as usual, she completed the job, which happened to be a very big house with a demanding lady of the house.

Grandmother was paid, she got her coat, purse and left. It was not until she got all the way back home, that she realized the lady of the house had stolen the money out of Grandmother's purse and paid her with her own money! It was a $10 bill. Grandmother had done all of that work for free! The money she had counted on to take care of her children and herself had been taken away from her and there was nothing she could do about it! Grandmother never returned to the big house again. This story was told to me by Grandmother some 30 years later and even as a child I could see the hurt and frustration in her eyes.

 When Grandmother "retired" she became a traveling woman! She traveled all over the country to attend the conferences and conventions of the church world. She and her artistry made it to almost all of the 50 states. She found her niche and created a world that was pleasing to her and for her. I had to cross the threshold of 50 to capture this level of wisdom.

The Balloon Sisters

Grandmother had 2 sisters in the area, the rest of her family remained in Florida and Georgia. She was very close to her sisters. They did not resemble each other at all, yet there were like 3 peas in a pod. As a child I was not privy to their conversations, for children were to be "seen and not heard." Adults did not discuss their affairs in the presence of children back then. The two worlds were intentionally separate and the boundaries kept well! Yet I could see the love of the three sisters and how they supported one another. The 3 sisters were not only different in appearance, their personalities were also quite different: Grandmother was quite reserved, stoic, methodical. Sister #1 was very thin, shy, quiet, spoke with a soft sweet voice like cotton candy. Whenever you saw her, you just wanted to hug her and get some of the sweetness.

Sister #2 was an intuitive thinker. She always looked like she knew some things that most did not-- short, round, curvy, bubbly and always smiling. Sisters 1 and 2 lived together all my coming up years until I went to middle school. Neither of them married or had children. When Sister #1 became ill, Sister #2 was still working and evidently the 3 peas in a pod decided they should live together to ensure Sister #1 could be looked after by my Grandmother. They moved into my Grandmother's home and remained together until my Grandmother's death some years later. These women were a unit, a model of quiet resilience and strength. They kept to themselves and lived a stealth life.

Now I unveil unto you...some of Grandmother's secrets.

Acutely Aware of one's environment: "God Bless!"

Grandmother had a code word, that everyone in our family knew the meaning. I can't quite remember when I "absorbed" the word, it just seemed like I just always knew. Whenever Grandmother used this word it meant the environment was no longer safe to continue the conversation the adults had been engaging in. Either someone had entered the room that was not trustworthy/gossiped (usually the case), did not need to hear about the topic, or it was none of their business.

I can remember as a child a room full of adults talking about whatever suited them, the room being lively and animated with all kind of gestures, laughter, questions and seem like out of nowhere you could hear Grandmother say "God Bless" and the entire room would go silent! Not another word would be spoken on the matter and everyone, including us children took note to our surroundings—who had just walked in the door? What was going on? Those 2 words were like the precursor for activation of the fight-flight mindset for my kin.

Grandmother did not have a loud robust voice, but it was something about the tone, that made us all aware of our environment. It was as though she was holding up a sign that said—SHUT UP AND PAY ATTENTION! From the knee baby to the oldest elder in the room, we all responded accordingly. The conversation seamlessly flowed in a completely opposite direction and the untrustworthy one was none the wiser.

Whenever I heard Grandmother sound the alarm with those words, I took note and stored the information for later. I knew there was something about an individual, group, or a change in the environment that had suddenly happened and I needed to stay alert and I did. It was not something that anyone ever talked about, even after the incident. It just was…

I passed this principle on to my children without giving it a second thought and more than likely they have done their own variation with their children. I have also shared it with a couple of close friends. There have been times when it has been so handy to say something that is socially accepted, yet has a totally different meaning for those in the know. The meaning is the same as the Spanish phrase "Cierra la boca!" Many awkward moments could be spared if we all were a little more alert and aware of our environments, to know when to not say anything further.

The Value of Knowing What to Keep Private: "tell some, keep some."

"Tell some, keep some." This was one of my grandmother's favorite phrases. Grandmother did not say a lot, but she wasn't exactly shy either. She was just one to make her words few, but effective. She was not one to be caught in the "gossip circle" or being a "busy-body." I never knew her name to come up in any sort of conflict.

She exemplified keeping focus on your own goals and intent. She never boasted or bragged about how she was going to do this or that, she just did her thing in a seamless way.

She believed that information had boundaries/compartments: general information, miscellaneous information, business information, and private information. These categories were forever separate…

This is such a sacred principle to embrace. Some of your information should remain private, not everything should be shared, not even with close family and friends. There are many private matters which should remain with you and the God of your understanding and acceptance. When private matters are indiscriminately shared, you cannot take it back. In the instant communication world of the internet, texting, IM, FB, Twitter and the like, it often seems like people have forgotten to "tell some, keep some." Not every comment, opinion, picture, description or conversation is appropriate for public domain. In the moment, what may seem like a funny gag, off-comment, or even letting off steam; may later come back and be used against you or someone you know; affecting employment, relationships, advancement and the like.

Yes there are times, when you can let your hair down, have some fun, "tell it like it is." This principle teaches you to distinguish the time, place and people—BEFORE, you let it all out! Trying to back-peddle or pull out your mop and bucket-AFTER-THE-FACT, can be quite embarrassing, time-consuming, frustrating, and even debilitating sometimes. We all have experienced, telling the wrong person personal information and it's later used against us! It is not a good feeling to say the least.

Sometimes it is not the information given out, per se, but the volume or quantity of information given out. For example, deep traumas, medical issues, mental health issues are generally not conversations to embark on with an acquaintance or someone you've recently met. There's not enough relationship history available yet to know if this is someone "safe" to share this level of information or can this person handle the topic, etc. When in doubt…don't share. Some information should be shared in small increments, to give the other person time to ingest what's been said and also to give you time to find out how much information is appropriate for this setting.

This principle teaches us to create filters for ourselves, that we may know what information remains private…what's available for the chosen-few…and what can be allowed into public domain. Remember to "tell some, keep some."

Know when to let go of the past.

Grandmother lived in the same house on 3rd Street all of my coming up years, until I went to high school. Her neighborhood to me was as familiar as breathing; the bakery across the street with all the exquisite smells of baking bread and rolls, the rows of white trucks parked in front of the bakery, neighbors, close proximity of the houses, the trees and shape of the street lights-- I could see it all with my eyes closed.

Grandmother's neighborhood always had the *feel* of comfort, good food cooking nearby, and heavenly scents of all different types of flowers in the back yards from Spring all the way up to late Fall. She lived on a wide street, with little traffic except for the bakery trucks and the neighbors. The street was wide enough to have cars parked on both sides of the street and still have plenty of room to drive.

Grandmother lived about 2 or 3 blocks away from the family church. She sometimes walked to the weekly afternoon prayer meeting along with a few neighbors. On the way back home she would stop by the corner store to get her favorite candy in the tin box and her Luden original cough drops.

Slowly but surely, Grandmother's old neighborhood began to change; the old neighbors died off, their adult children sold the properties and moved away and the bakery closed down. As the neighborhood changed, many of the local businesses downsized or closed down too. By the time I was a teen, the neighborhood was no longer safe for the older ones to live by themselves. The Gate Keepers of the rhythms and sounds of the neighborhood had almost all faded away...

I was not privy to what all took place for Grandmother to move from her spacious house to a 2 bedroom apartment on the other side of town. I just remember my first visit to the new place. It was an upstairs apartment with no smell of baking bread or sweet flowers. It was about 1/3 of the space of the old house. I did not know any of the neighbors and there was nowhere to just be—as it had been in the ole neighborhood. The new place was on a much busier street with people closer to my parents' age or just a little older than me. They seemed unfriendly (in comparison to the old neighborhood) and had no connection to Grandmother or my family.

Grandmother couldn't walk to church if she chose to, as she had been able to do before; she would have to catch 2 buses or arrange for someone to pick her up. All of these thoughts were swirling around in my teenage head, but I knew better than to voice them. *I didn't like the new place at all!* It was too different, too small, too much change all at once. I wanted the old house back!

Grandmother had fixed up the place beautiful with all her colorful pillows, doilies, antique furniture, flower arrangements and beautiful oriental and persian rugs. With a keen eye I watched Grandmother to see if I could tell, if she felt as I did about the new place. There was no look of pain, sadness or frustration on her face and I really looked hard to see if it was there. She never mentioned what she had to give up, to fit into the apartment, how she missed the old neighbors and habits or anything that would have shown she was not content. She simply made us all a cup of tea.

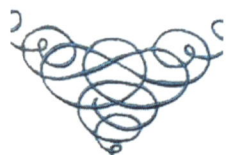

 *Whatever you do...Do it with Excellence!*

My Grandmother's best friend was our Beloved "Babe." I talk about the many things Babe and her husband, "Dad" provided for me as a child in my first book, *I Found My Voice* (www.lulu.com;Amazon) Babe was in her 80's when I was born. She was 5' 8", brown- like - pecans, with a slight shadowing of a moustache which she never shaved and she was easily, over 300 lbs. She had a firm voice, mixed with tenderness. She was my Godmother AND my father's Godmother. She took care of me, while my parents worked until I became school age. It was one of the most loving environments I have ever experienced, until this day! As I began to look back, some 50 years later the gifts become even more precious and tender, for I am awakening to what I was actually seeing way back then. I now have the honor of bringing those principles into my Now and sharing it with others. Babe had also been a "Day's Worker", meaning she cleaned the houses of the rich White folks in the surrounding suburbs. By the time I came along, she no longer worked outside the home, yet she worked and earned money all the time…

The rich people came from near and far to have Babe do their laundry and iron their clothes. Her system was probably 50 or 60 years old by then. She got up early in the morning, hung the clothes out on the line at first sun with wooden clothes pins. The clothes blew in the breeze and warmth of the sun, even when it was cold.

She made her own starch from a powdered mix of Argo, Corn Starch, and another blue liquid product I've long forgotten. She knew the exact water - powder ratio to get the clothing to look like they had been professionally ironed by a dry cleaners. She had an old fashioned iron with a black and white cloth cord. It looked like it was, one step removed from when you had to heat the iron on the stove.

Babe always did her ironing in the "sitting room" while she watched her "stories" on the 17" black and white TV which remained the Only TV in her beautiful home until I was an adult. I think her children later bought her a 24" color one, but her favorite was still the 17" one. She had her system—rows of baskets separated by items and customers, wired hangers, and a big hooks on the back of the cellar door for her to hang the clothes up, as she finished.

If she noticed a missing or loose button on the pristine white business shirts, a loose hem line on a dress or some minor repair work needed; she took out one of her "sewing kits", which were large pretty tins that had once held Christmas fruit cake. They now held every imaginable color of thread and size needle. Most importantly, were the "thimbles." She had rubber thimbles, silver thimbles, of all different sizes. She always used a thimble when she was sewing.

She had natural breaks that she would take and she would cook me and Dad food fit for Kings and Queens. Oh! Could she cook. Sometimes she'd stop and visit with friends in the neighborhood, who would stop by. She always had plenty to share and lived a full life, before my young eyes.

Her house was always Peaceful and had a certain synergy and rhythm.

Her attention to detail and her excellent service, caused her to be paid well. How do I know, although I never actually saw the exchange of money; I could tell both the "customer" and Babe were pleased and there was a light-hearted spirit of satisfaction in the air.

Although I was not consciously aware of it at the time, I used these principles my grandmother and Babe taught me regularly when I became an adult. One of those times was when I moved to a new state and was looking for a job. I was trained, certified, had plenty of experience and a college degree. I thought it would be relatively easy to find a job. The economy was good, I anticipated I would have a job any day. Well…any day seem to turn into many days of being turned down because I "didn't have experience in this state." I thought to myself if you hire me, I will. I continued in my job search for months with the same response.

I had worked in group homes for the mentally ill early on in my career, so when I saw an ad that had an opening not far from where I lived, I applied and got the job. It paid minimum wage. They got a highly experienced person for minimum wage, I got my foot in the door. It was a beautiful home with 4 men who had been institutionalized most of their lives, now transitioning into the community. Until another woman and I were hired, it had been staffed by all men, usually college students who needed the flexibility of working various shifts on different days.

One of the things I noticed I could help with, my first day there was the linen closet in the clients' rooms were totally disorganized—towels and sheets mixed together, sheet sets not put together; everything sort of balled up on the shelf. I suggested to my co-worker we start the day by organizing the linen closets; I took the 2 back rooms and she took the front rooms. They were large closets and it took a couple of hours to pair the sheets up, put the wash cloths together, hand towels, and towels in an orderly fashion.

The first room's resident was a man severely developmentally delayed, mentally ill, and had limited verbal communication skills. After completing the morning routine of the shift, I began to organize the closet. Before I started I asked him would he like for me to organize his linen closet and he said yes. His bedroom window faced the back yard and always got the first sun. I began my task with the sun shining through his window and a picture of lush green grass growing in the back yard. I was happy to be employed and to be able to give service in this simplistic way.

When I finished I showed him how organized the linen closet was and where everything belonged; he clapped his hands. I was told a week later by staff, he always pulled the linen off the shelves and left it on the floor, as though he was angry(?!) It was surprising to the staff, once the closet was organized, he stopped that behavior. He did not pull the linen off the shelves, the entire time I worked there. The rest of the staff followed suit and kept the linen closet organized. Maybe he was just trying to get someone to organize his closet...

Excellence is a better teacher than mediocrity. The lessons of the ordinary are everywhere. Truly profound and original insights are to be found only in studying the exemplary. Warren G. Bennis

There were other simplistic things that I did on my shifts that made it comfortable for the clients and practical for my co-workers. Everyone was so appreciative of the extra help, suggestion, and organization.... Within 30 days of working at the group home, I got a $2.00/hr. raise; 2 weeks after that I got a bonus. Two weeks after the raise + the bonus, a management position became available at the main office, when I told my supervisor I was going to apply for the position; she called the owner of the company and told her to go ahead and put an ad in the paper for the group home position, because my work was excellent and I would get the job! I did get the job and 2 weeks after I got the management job, I got a management raise; two weeks later I got another bonus. In less than 4 months, I went from minimum wage to multiple raises, bonuses and a management position.

   I worked in excellence at minimum wage, which opened the door for me to work in excellence in a management position. Having worked in the group home first, gave me the insight I needed to really know what the direct service people, I would later supervise, had to do and deal with on their shifts. I learned the personality, challenges, and specific melt-downs each client could have and how to assist them to get stable again. Because of the caring hard work of the staff, none of the clients were hospitalized. I got to see what it takes to have that kind of record.

         The information I received, as a minimum wage employee was priceless and a necessary step, for the next rung of the ladder! When I became a manager, every now and then a staff person was sick or had a family emergency and could not work their shift. If another staff was not available, as the Supervisor I would have to cover that shift. Going back into the group home during those times was easy-breezy, because I already knew the lay of the land. I knew each of the clients and their routine, including medications. Most importantly, the clients knew me, I was not a disturbance to their natural rhythms.

         We need to internalize this idea of excellence. Not many folks spend a lot of time trying to be excellent. President Barack Obama

I learned from Grandmother and Babe, how to do things with excellence and the harvest has always been beyond what I could have imagined! Always! This mindset of having excellence of mind, spirit, and actions is not readily embraced in our micro-wave-culture. Seems like, most people are always in a Rush to get Somewhere Else! Too Busy-Too Busy-Too Busy! Too busy for customer service, too busy to say Good Morning to a neighbor, Too busy to offer a helping hand, too busy to eat, sleep, and play well. Anything that does not have an automatic projection to the next level or getting in front of the "*right people,*" or bringing instant material wealth is not readily cheered or embrace by society as a whole, especially western culture.

The nuggets, gifts, lessons, comfort, warnings, information and "data" of the Now is *Often* rejected, minimalized, dismissed, missed, overlooked, and pushed away for the *perceived* better.

I had the same skills when I was hired for the minimum wage job as I had when they hired me for the management job; the only difference was they had experienced it for themselves. I didn't need job references when I applied for the management position, everyone who had experienced my work from the clients to the supervisor could and did speak for me. The owner of the company knew of my work, before we ever met. My reputation of excellence spoke for itself~

I did not have a game plan of how I would impress people and they would put in a good word for me. I went to work in Gratitude and did what I saw needed to, be done. I did not spend my time focusing on all the things I did not want such as the minimum pay or entry level position. I focused on all the wonderful things about this opportunity. I worked in a beautiful setting, I was working in my field of mental health, I got to see the various stages of each client's diagnosis and how they responded to this new environment-this was very interesting and informative to me. I worked less than 7 miles from where I lived, which allowed me to lay in bed an extra 15 -20 minutes because I didn't have to worry about traffic or gas; which is an extra delight for someone who is not a morning person!

For me there was so much to be grateful for and I knew the other stuff would work itself out. If I had went to work every day in angst and frustration about the position, if I had done mediocre work because I was angry about being there—thinking I'll do excellent work when I get a higher position, if I had treated the clients and my co- workers otherwise than respectful--I never would have received all the bounty and prosperity, which came out of my applying for a minimum wage job~

Excellence is to do a common thing in an uncommon way.

Booker T. Washington

I have a few favorite thrift stores that I like to rummage through, for me it's always like a treasure hunt. On days that have been really stressful at work, it is a welcomed free therapeutic exercise to look at the books, see if anything catches my eye or the antique furniture, lamps—which always takes me back to my own childhood memories. I was recently at one of my stores, sitting in an antique chair sorting through my buggy, deciding what would make the final cut of going home with me.

A woman came up, inquiring about an office chair to one of the employees who had been organizing the electronics on the shelf. He told her about every aspect of the chair that he knew, including a couple of flaws. He mentioned because it was an antique it would require a specific kind of screw to sit up correctly. He went on to say, the screws may have fallen out when the chair was being placed. He preceded to, get on his hands and knees and look under all the pieces of furniture to see if the screws could be found.

When he could not find any screws, he told the woman to leave her contact info with the cashier and if he found the screws he would contact her and she could return to the store, to get the screws. He also told her a specific hardware store in the area that might still carry those particular screws. The woman was so pleased for all the "extra" information she received and gladly purchased the chair. There were several other customers who received this same level of attention to detail from this employee, while I was in the area. If he did not know the answer, he went to get someone who had the answer. Each customer was well satisfied and purchased multiple items from that area. This employee doesn't get commission for what sells, he didn't know I had overheard his service to the customers, he was just being himself.

When I finished sorting through my loot, I went over to him and I thanked him for how he served each of those customers and the level of detail he gave to each of their needs or requests. I went further and told him, if I owned the store, he is the kind of employee I would want working in my business. He was very grateful for the encouragement and responded by saying, "you can go many days before someone says thank you or any kind words for the work you do."

As I was thanking him for what he had given the other customers, there was a man in close proximity to us, who was intently listening and watching as the employee and I talked. His intent look caused me to glance over at him. He looked utterly astonished that I would take the time to thank the employee for providing service to others. He continued to listen to us talk, until I walked away. For whatever reason, he too was exposed to the circle of excellence and I trust, he will one day pass it on too.

Although the employee did not wait on me, specifically, I was still positively impacted by his spirit of excellence and today I write about it. Having received such a feast for eyes and ears, I had to complete the circle by allowing him to know his work was appreciated and did make a difference. He in turn, was encouraged to continue on in a spirit of excellence.

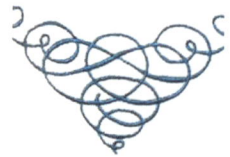

The Joy of Creating a Beautiful Home

I remember the warmth of walking into my Grandmother's home, there was a long hallway and then you turned to the left to go into the living-room. Every nook and cranny expressed her personality and interests—knick knacks, flower vases, linen tablecloths and colorful cushioned furniture, beautiful curtains and doilies. As beautiful and neat as it was, it had a certain feeling—it felt homey. She had the most beautiful china plates, glasses and cups. Some of the cups and glasses were trimmed in gold, around the rim. As a child I loved to see the beautiful colors.

It is the teachings of the Moors that color stimulates brain activity and creativity. Grandmother demonstrated that to me without saying a word. Each room had its own assortment of themes and decorations. She was quite the interior decorator. Her house always felt pretty and magical. I would imagine all kinds of things whenever we went to visit her.

This taught me that my space should be soothing to my heart and my eyes! That whenever I return home, there should be a smile from within, that comes from my toes all the way up to my stimulated mind; that coming home should always feel like a warm embrace, shelter and protection from the onslaught of the outside world. That my nerve endings should dance and have a sigh of relief—*for I Am Home!*

When I look around my own home, I see a lot of Grandmother within my expressions. I too have cushiony furniture with colorful pillows, lamps of different sizes and shapes, crystal candleholders, and lace curtains—just to name a few. I also have other things that are solely my own individual expression. When I look around my home, I see me in every nook and cranny. To this day my home is my *Favorite* place to be. It is where I center, create, relax, and tap into my inner being. It is the one place that I can be fully me without any parameters or restraints, *I Am Home!*

The Alchemy of Home

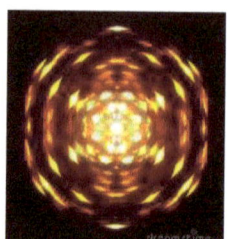

Grandmother's house was so full of wonder and creativity that at the age of 4, my father became a musical protégée. One day while Grandmother and her friend Babe were in the kitchen having tea, they heard music coming from the "parlor." When they went to see what was going on, they saw my father sitting at the piano, playing a song with complex chords. The women were extremely surprised and excited, because their newly established church was in desperate need of a musician and my father had never showed interest in playing the piano prior to that day! It was 1936. The church was able to gain many visitors, who stayed and became members, as a result of the gifted child musician, who could play any song a person began to sing. It did not matter if it was an ole family tune, a revered hymn, or a spontaneous song—he could play them all!

Those were hard times for Black families trying to survive the geographical transition from the farmland of the South to urban life in the North. Their lives were often impacted by poverty, racism, untreated medical issues and lack of resources. It was their building of *community* which allowed them to survive, provide for their children, and work long hours doing hard labor. Most of the church-goers could not read, as it was not allowed on the plantations and farms of the south where the majority had migrated from. Even the Pastor, could only read the Bible, as a result of prayer to be able to do so. It was soothing, uplifting, and encouraging, to have their spiritual experiences, enhanced with music from a child, who had been given the gift of music. Many saw this as a sign that God would see them through those hard times and they often gave thanks for the child on the piano, playing one of their favorite songs.

When I was a teen my father told me how he became a musician, he said the next day after he played the first song; "*I saw all the musical chords in my head and I knew I could play them, so I did.*" From that day on, whenever he heard music on the radio that he liked, he went to the piano and played it. It did not matter whether it was gospel, jazz, blues, or classical, if he heard it and liked it he could play it! He never had a lesson and could not read music, but he played music unlike any other musician, at that time. In his teens, my father became interested in playing an organ. He convinced his church to buy an old organ and he taught himself to play the organ. By the time I came along, he had his favorite instruments—a *Wurlitzer piano* and a *Hammond organ*. We had a *Wurlitzer* piano in our home, my entire life.

My father was often sought out for recording professionally, but he always turned it down because of his religious beliefs. He did not believe it was acceptable to play secular music and be a Christian in good standing. This was prior to the birth of Gospel music and traditional "church music" did not have a following large enough to interest record companies. He followed the convictions of his heart and his understanding of the tenets of his faith. He chose to live the life of a state employee, living in middle class, rather than the status and material wealth of a recording artist. This was a choice both my parents made, as my mother was a phenomenal singer and the two together was something awesome to hear! There are times in life when big Decisions must be made and the authentic self is called upon to stand. How we respond to the call, will greatly impact our lives and demonstrate the Law of Cause and Effect.

I remember one time, when I was in the 9th grade my parents went to the music store to look at new pianos. While there, my father played one of his songs on the most expensive piano in the store, the owner of the store rushed over to my father and offered him a record deal on the spot! He tried his best to convince my father, the record business had changed and he would not have to play music that he did not want to play. He offered to sell my father the expensive piano at the price of the least expensive piano, along with all the other amenities of being a recording artist. My father declined his offer. The music store owner insisted that my parents take his business cards—*just in case my father changed his mind.* As usual, my father turned it down. My parents returned home giddy and excited about how the music store owner and all the other people in the store made such a big deal about the way my father played his song on that expensive piano. They laughed and talked about the excitement for the rest of the night.

My father, went on to train and organize, some of the best soloists and choirs in his region. His peers, nick-named him, "Professor Keys", because of what he did *with* the keys! There were many he taught who became famous Gospel singers and musicians. My father chose to remain a well-established gospel musician, songwriter, composer, and singer throughout his state and church organization.

Sometimes on Saturdays, if the church was being cleaned, rehearsals were at my home and I had a first-class-seat for some of the best music and songs you would ever want to hear! They usually practiced 2 – 4 hours, until every note, every tone, and all the harmony was precise. There were times, when the music and the singing would get so good/be in synch that the musicians and the singers would "get happy"—meaning they would become so in tuned with the words of the song and incorporate it, with their own experiences, that they would begin to cry, rejoice, lift up their hands and say—"Thank you Lord!" If a phrase of the song was...*my soul looks back and wonders how I got over...* or there would come *a time when– I won't have to cry no more...*everyone in the room could relate to these words! These were second generation northerners who had known challenging times and were just starting to turn the corner on getting a slice of the American pie.

Many of the songs that were sung on Sundays at the church were written and arranged by my father. He was an awesome song writer and composer. He had both an "ear" and an "eye" for music; whichever way the soloists or the choir director went with the song, he could follow, accentuate certain parts and take it right back to the chorus.

It has taken me 5 decades to become aware of the *Alchemy* that was my everyday life, as a child. Seeing my father and mother with the choirs during rehearsals, taught me so much more than how to sing and keep time. It demonstrated the spirit of excellence, community, spirituality, connections, unity, commitment, dedication and a wealth of other things I am just beginning to realize and acknowledge.

Music in Black churches is very much a part of the service and a good musician knows how to follow the flow of what is taking place at the time—to know when the music should be soft and sacred, loud and expressive, or just a few chords here and there is the work of a seamless musician and my father was one of the greatest! All of this was possible because my father grew up in a home that was chock full of *Alchemy*. How else could it have been possible for a 4 year old Black male child, in 1936, who had just lost his father the year before, be able to *hear the music and go to the piano and play it*. How did his widow mother think to have a piano in her house, when she did not play the piano? Where did she get the resources to get the piano, have it delivered and set up in her parlor? ALCHEMY!

Home is meant to be the place where creativity, awakenings, birthings, deaths, rejuvenation, new ideas, changes, solitude, play and destiny have full expressions.

Home is meant to be to the person, what the heart is to the body. Without the heart, the body cannot function, it ceases to exist! Without living in the true essence of home, we too cease to exist. We become drones—the walking dead, predictable pawns—waiting for someone else to tell us who to be/what to like/how to live.

In the fast-paced-world of movers and shakers, some folks have forgotten that their home is not to be a show-piece, status symbol, or decorated to impress the visitors more than to serve and soothe the ones who live within. The triune of your personhood needs the natural ebb and flow of action time and rest time. The body cannot function at its optimum when all your days are 16, 18, 20 hour days—for years on end. The mind cannot function at a right-functioning-capacity when old thoughts, un-digested thoughts, and new data are all vying for the same head-space. As much as you may enjoy a vacation to an exotic resort, stand proud for the accolades of business or career success…there truly is No Place Like Home.

The spirit of man cannot lead or intuit if it is not regularly fed with soulful activities such as meditation or yoga. Every aspect of your being cries out in some way to go home on a regular basis. That home is your physical residence and your inner residence…Dare I ask when was the last time you were *still* enough in your home for a creative idea/thought/action/invention to come to you? The sub conscious mind is always full of new ideas/activities/plans…it takes *stillness* for what is in the subconscious mind to make its way across the barriers to the conscious mind; only through this process do we become *AWARE*

What shows up in the conscious mind as a brand new thing, has usual been sitting in the unconscious realm for quite some time...

 *When you walk in your door, does your home greet you or make a grand display of who you are, to the outside world? When was the last time you were really home?*

Aim: It is my desire to begin and end each day in the true essence and nature of being home, in tuned with the divine. Everything in my internal and external home aligns with the harmony and balance of home and

I AM COMPLETE NOW!

The Spirit of Excellence

A Spirit of Excellence resonates at a person's core and everything they touch has the glow. It is *Heart-Centered and everyone who comes in contact is influenced by it.* A Spirit of Excellence comes with the *Sole* intent of giving without expectation of personal gain or status. It gives of itself because it is the right thing to do—it is who they are! A Spirit of Excellence is different from accomplishing a specific goal by doing expected or necessary tasks in a way which brings recognition and accolades. Neither it is it the work of the exhausted perfectionist.

A Spirit of Excellence isn't about what-you-should-do Or what-you-gotta-do Or what-you're-expected-do Or what-you-do-when someone's-watching-you; it is the most natural thing for an individual with this gift—they act with integrity. It is the nature and essence of the person to give honorable service to others. A Spirit of Excellence does not have a particular tenet of faith…may not necessarily belong to a prestigious organization…or be on first-name-basis with the movers and shakers.

The spirit of excellence is just about *be-ing who you are*, showing up as an expression of divinity when a situation presents itself. Although a Spirit of Excellence can be a great leader and motivate people and do it very well; they often *prefer* to be behind the scenes taking care of all the little details that must be done to make things happen and be successful.

A Spirit of Excellence lives in the home of the 4th Chakrah. The 4th Chakrah is Heart Energy. It is the center of the major 7 Chakrahs. Chakrahs are spinning energy wheels, which are connected to the physical body and emotions. Each Chakrah has life lessons and initiations which must be passed to get to the next stage in life. A Spirit of Excellence vibrates on the color Green. Dark green leafy vegetables, iodine, iron, grains, legumes and are favorable contributors to this vibration according to the teachings of the ancient Egyptian Sages.

The Sanskrit name for this chakra is Anahata, meaning unstuck or unhurt. To open the heart is to treat others (as well as things) with honor and respect and refrain from causing unnecessary harm. This occurs naturally when we discover the divine nature of the self within and realize that a similar nature resides within others and indeed all of life. An open heart feels compassion and empathy for both self and others. It understands the tender nature of spirit, the delightful joy of connection, and the deep peace of acceptance. The heart's task is to find balance in relationships in all aspects: mind and body, self and other, light and shadow, masculine and feminine, inner and outer realms. The result of this balance is peace.

Anodea Judith, Chakra Balancing Workbook

The fourth chakra is located in the center of the chest and rules over the lungs, heart, pericardium, upper back and ribs, inner arms and hands. It relates to the respiratory system and breath.

Anodea Judith, Chakra Balancing Workbook

To open this chakra is to dissolve the illusion of separateness and the needs of the ego. It is to open yourself to loving more deeply and to falling in love with life itself. Ultimately, this chakra begins a passionate love affair with divine spirit and all of its infinitely perfect manifestations.

Anodea Judith, Chakra Balancing Workbook

Part II: The 9 Aspects of "Being Home"

There are 9 Aspects of "Being Home."

1. Body-temple-Home
2. Thought-sanctuary-Home
3. Spiritual Home
4. Emotional Home
5. Community Home
6. Money Home
7. Passion Home
8. Courage Home
9. Trust Home

There are 3 Initiation Points in the 9 Aspects of "Being Home":

Initiation I: Earthen Vessel

    Body - Temple Home

    Thought - Sanctuary Home

    Spiritual Home

Initiation II: Self Alignment

    Emotional home

    Community home

    Money home

Initiation III: The Connection of Zebra Medicine

    Passion Home

    Courage Home

    Trust Home

INITIATION I: Earthen Vessel

Body - Temple Home

Thought - Sanctuary Home

Spiritual Home

The Initiation of the Earthen Vessel is about "being grounded" in one's own body, mind, spirit; to know oneself in an intimate way—the good, the bad, the ugly; the positive and negative aspects, the light and the dark sides. It is the initiation of finding peace with oneself, giving up the ego's dominion of comparing oneself to others and their *perceived* better circumstances. It is the honor, acknowledgment, respect, and thanksgiving for the Vessel that you are; to be able to grasp one's own greatness and have the willingness to let your own light shine at the divine capacity you have been given. It is the *Full Acceptance* of the *essence* of divinity that you are! There will never be another Y-O-U. You are divinely, uniquely, and wonderfully made. *All of life's potentials lie within you!* Just as within the mustard seed and the acorn are their destinies. Neither one of these seeds look too great or much to talk about, in their beginning stages, but give them some time and you will be looking up at them!

You are *of* the earth and *of* the divine, 2 aspects united within the physical earthen vessel; a clay container with limitless capability. *As the clay must go through the fire to become fit for use, so must you. This fire is not meant to destroy you…it is meant to mold, shape and preserve you; to bring out the best of you as you capture the wisdom of this initiation.*

An *Initiation* is the steps, decisions, actions which lead you on your path of life. It is always up to the earthen vessel which direction it makes a *decision* to go into. The opinions, beliefs, behavior patterns and other personality traits we portray often lead us back to our family of origin patterns. It is up to the earthen vessel during this Initiation Period to become the explorer within to determine what tools are useful and which ones are broken or no longer appropriate for the next part of the journey.

The Life lessons for the Earthen Vessel are presented in a myriad of ways, daily. Almost every encounter is subtly lined with the questions: Which way will you go? Why do you choose that response/path/decision? For an example an unexpected situation presents itself, will you have an ego-response or will you take the high road? Will you show compassion or will you go for the jugler? All Energy is cyclical...what we give/send out...Must return to us...that Is the Law.

Sometimes our deep-seated issues find hideaways in our subconscious mind and we have not given permission for the issues to come to our awareness in our conscious mind. This is how we attract circumstances which repeatedly *show* us what we are unwilling to face. The intensity of the circumstances is beckoning to us to become Aware of the Lessons and move forward with Wisdom. This is the purpose and destiny of the Earthen Vessel Initiation Season and Rhythm of Life.

Body Temple Home

To be present in your Body Temple Home, is to have peace, satisfaction and acceptance about the physical body; to be free of the need to compare your body temple with any other body temple; to recognize the sacredness of your body temple, for it is the container, the vessel, which houses your spirit and emotions; to be fully attuned with your own body; to be fully present in your body; to know your body in every way.

For example, can you answer these questions without hesitation: When I get angry/happy/sad my physical body responds by _____ and I feel the emotion in my_____; when I feel that physical response in my body I know for sure I am_____. I respond/do not respond/ignore this physical message from my body.

For example: When I think about my physical body
I_____.

The Aim: I daily treat my body with loving care, tenderness, understanding, and acceptance. I thank my kin and kine for all the attributes, characteristics, and expressions that are uniquely mine. I honor my body-temple-home with gratitude and thanksgiving for life.

>   *My Body*
>
> *How do I balance the books with my body?*
>
> *It has remained faithful and true under all circumstances.*
>
> *Whatever state I was in, my body was there too.*
>
> *It was there as a perfect size x*
>
> *And it was there at what I considered a defeated size xx.*
>
> *My heart has been beating for 365 days straight?*
>
> *My lungs have continued to take in and expel oxygen.*
>
> *My legs have walked near and far.*
>
> *My kidneys, my liver, my intestines work non-stop,*
>
> *without recognition or appreciation.*

My eyes, nose and mouth have Never forgotten their function,

even when I have forgotten mine!

If my body was an employee, would a gold watch suffice

for the years of service?

How about a bonus? Stock options? A Promotion?

Company car-perhaps?

What would be an adequate repayment for such loyalty?

Today I honor my body and bow in gratitude.

K. Mhina Entrantt, ©2009

Thought Sanctuary Home

It is reported the average person has over 70,000 thoughts a day. Some research says up to 80% of these thoughts are negative and repetitive. The exact same thoughts we had yesterday, we often allow to dominate our Today and the Now. We are captivated by thoughts entrenched in worry, negativity, regrets about the past, and a variety of fears.

We too often allow our mind to become like the old attic or dark basement where all kind of things have been dumped, discarded, and stored. The mind has become so FULL of old stuff, that there is hardly any room for new thoughts, new ideas, new plans, enthusiasm and inspiration to get in the door. We have forgotten how to be good stewards over our own thoughts. We have allowed the Past to dominate our mind.

We have allowed What-ifs to keep us stagnant. We have allowed the opinions of others to keep us *STUCK*. Our thoughts are only sporadically *in the present moment*. We have habitually become more outer-centered than inner-centered. If we are not careful, we will hand our thoughts over to other people, media, social status symbols and our family-tribe. We will have a semblance of life, but never have truly *lived.* To actually live within the Thought sanctuary Home, we must release the past episodes of our lives and create mental space for new ideas, creations, observations, experiences and people that are awaiting your beckoning call. By the affirmative thoughts you think on a consistent basis.

For example, all the men/women in your family-tribe for the last 3 generations have been in career/trade X; you have a Passion for career/trade Y, which one will you choose? Why?

For example, you meet someone who you absolutely enjoyed talking to and would love to go on the date they've asked you on, but you know they will not pass your family/friends/social groups' approval because of the person's physical appearance, status, income-what will you do? Why?

For example, a great opportunity has opened up for you to pursue your passion and be well paid too. You remember the last time you took a chance on something and it did not turn out as you expected, fear of the unknown and old anxieties began to surface-What will you do? Why?

Suppose!
Suppose the world was a safe place just waiting for the real you to come forward.
Suppose there really was still time left, for you to live your dreams outrageously!
Suppose everything you ever desired was truly obtainable.
Suppose the love of your life was already in your life and you were enjoying it all.
Suppose money was no problem, you always had more than enough.
Suppose everything you're worrying about was already resolved.
Suppose your best days were before you and not behind you.
Suppose you were free from the things that use to keep you down.

Suppose it's true, then what?

K. Mhina Entrantt, ©2009

Spiritual Home

If you asked the average person about spirituality, they would tell you about their *religion* and the tenets or dogma of that particular religion or they may say I don't go to church/have a religion. Although spirituality and religion can have some parallel concepts, traditions, or rituals they are *not* the same. Spirituality refers to being attuned to the divine essence of life itself, as purely seen when we pay attention to nature and aspire to live by the laws of nature. A bird sings, because it was made to sing. A blade of grass grows as it was meant to grow. The sun rises and sets on us all. The moon waxes, wanes, and goes through all the other cycles effortlessly. The law of gravity is always working.

Spirituality is laced with Gratitude, Appreciation for simple, everyday experiences, and the Acknowledgement of the necessity to sit in the silence of divine-essence: a slow walk on an autumn day, where you stop and appreciate nature's announcement of a new *season*-the turning of the leaves, their falling, the fading of the brilliant colors all around, the sound of crumbled, dark leaves under your feet. The willingness to capture that moment and hone in on what nature is showing you about the season of *your* life— *This is the voice of your spiritual home.* Is it your time to slow down, reflect, pay attention to detail, plan for the future? Do you need to take a break? Get some rest? Have some time alone?

Spirituality is in synch with the natural rhythms and cycles of the earth, ebb and flow of life, seed-time and harvest time. Your spiritual home is your keen awareness of your own rhythms and cycles. Just as we know it is autumn when we see the leaves changing colors, we must be able to identify what *season* it is in our own lives. *We must know the right timing for ourselves.* Is your physical and mental energies high in the morning, afternoon, or evening? Are you at your peak, brain-storming in a group or do you need solo time to process first? Do you have natural leadership skills or are you the detail person or maybe a little of both? Do you know who you are?

Your spiritual home is where you take off *all* the masks, all the half-truths, all the bartering, and the mundane feelings of emptiness that cannot be satisfied by material acquisitions. Even when you have the *rights-the right job, the right house, the right car, the right partner, the right money, the right friends, the right image, the right success as you define it…there will always be a lingering dissatisfaction if the spark of the divine is not continuously lit, from the inside out.*

For Example: Find a quiet place and close your eyes for 5 minutes, begin to empty your mind of all the concerns or happenings of the day. If you have not practiced being in the silence for awhile or have never done it before, the ego-mind will try to resist this new practice; all kind of thoughts will flood your mind at first. Don't become impatient or frustrated, just remain still and silent. Slowly, but surely, the thoughts will begin to fade and you begin to feel refreshed. Do this exercise twice a week, feel free to increase your time and frequency, as you see fit.

For Example: Take a nature walk, once a week; bring a pocket-size notebook and a pen with you. When something along your walk, catches your attention write it down. Close your eyes for a brief moment, take 3 breaths-fully inhaling and exhaling. Immediately take out your notebook and pen, write the first thing that comes to your mind for as long as you are *inspired* to write. Review what you have written during your nature walks, once a month. You will be *inspired* what to do next, honor what you are *inspired* to do with Action and Enthusiasm.

The Sacred
There is a place that I can go to when my mind is confused and my emotions are disheveled and my body is hurting.
There is a place that I can go to when my best seems like it's not good enough and I want to get off the treadmill of one disappointment after another.
There is a place that I can go to with a raggedy torn heart and promises of never trusting, never loving again!
There is a place where I am always loved and completely understood and outstretched arms await.
There is a place of such powerful silence that it sounds like thunder roaring and lightening crackling.
There is a place where my soul is at ease and I breathe deep sighs of peace.
This soft cushiony place lies within us all, waiting for recognition.
Can you feel it… see it yet? If you really want to, you will.
K. Mhina Entrantt ©2009

INITIATION II: *Self Alignment*

Emotional Home

Community Home

Money Home

The Initiation of Self Alignment

Self-Alignment is the ability to have integrity with oneself; to be in harmony with your thoughts, words, actions, decisions, hopes, dreams, desires, personal and business relationships. For example, your actions should match your decisions and your decisions should match your words. If you get in your car with the intent of traveling *North*, that is the direction you should be heading in. To find yourself going *East*, would be out of alignment with where you said you wanted to go. It does not matter how interesting, pretty, exciting, or different things may be on the road heading *East*, your intent was to head *North*, Unless you have changed your mind to travel *East, to find yourself traveling in any direction but North would be out of harmony and alignment of your stated intent!*

Anyone who has ever driven a car which was out of alignment knows how challenging and uncomfortable it is to try to steer and drive a car that's out of alignment. There is a resistance, a pulling in the opposite direction from what the driver is trying to do. It does not matter if the car is brand new or 20 years old, to be out of alignment is a malfunction and must be addressed and corrected. Certain functions of the car will still operate, although the car is out of alignment, but there will be a strain on the car's ability to operate at its full potential, as it was designed to do. As so, with hue-mans. You may still be able to work, pay bills, parent, travel, have relationships and have some form of spirituality, but you will not be capable of operating at your maximum potential when you are out of alignment.

We often do ourselves a disservice by being out of alignment with our words, actions, and decisions and become frustrated/annoyed/heart-broken/discouraged when the results and attractions in our lives do no match what we said we wanted or intended. It is IMPOSSIBLE to get *North Direction* miracles/blessings/benefits on an *East Direction* road. All of your help, people, money, and all good intended things and experiences are waiting for you to head in the right Direction and they will meet you there—actually they are already there, waiting on you and wondering why it's taking you so long! You must be in alignment with your *Destiny* to receive the *depth of Destiny* gifts, understanding, experiences and grounding; YOU MUST BE WALKING IN INTEGRITY WITH YOUR PURPOSE.

Alignment and purpose do not show up with a deep voice and thunder in the sky, it comes in drips and drops...little dots connecting. It comes through and with feelings of Peace and Love, you begin to feel a slight nudging from within to do a specific thing, read a book, go somewhere and the absolute best of circumstances begin to fall open, right before your eyes. Some call that a miracle...some call it synchronicity...some call it alchemy...we all can call it ...the state of being in alignment...

To be in alignment with Oneself, will cost you something; you may not be able to make all the social events if your studying for an exam, practicing for a sport, creating or planning. It may feel uncomfortable or like you're missing out, but your motivation comes through your alignment with yourself. You may be tempted every now and then, to not put your best foot forward so that you may have a chance to do what others are doing. If you succumb to the temptation, there are consequences to pay—for every action there is a reaction. Only you can decide how deep your Self Integrity is...

To have and hold Integrity with Oneself is the most important relationship possible within the hue-man experience. When we are out of alignment with ourselves, every aspect of our life will be off-centered. People will show up in your life and treat you, the way you think about yourself and how you treat yourself. If you allow the ego to rehearse your mistakes/mis-steps/blunders in your ear, more than you highlight your triumphs/celebrate all the little successes/pat yourself on the back, even when it doesn't quite turn out like you expect; you will find yourself surrounded by negative, critical, insensitive people-places-things. They have shown up to make you aware of how you, do-you.

If you have time to help everybody with their projects and crises, but never make time for your own self inventory or relaxation, that is the way others will deal with you also. If you realize that you often keep company with untruthful, untrustworthy family members, colleagues, friends or lovers; it is time to look for your, self - integrity leak! For this is a sure sign that you have one.

When we are in alignment with ourselves, everything else will fall in place or get out of the way for your intended good to come forth with full access. This is the Initiation of the Emotional House, Community House, and Money House.

Looking in the Mirror of Life!

I Stand here in this Mirror of Life
looking at/pondering/acknowledging
the Wombman, Queen, Evolved Being I've become
And my eyes begin to flood w/ tears.
For I know this moment has been hard won w/
blood/sweat/tears/fears
/disappointments/
sudden,
 unexpected endings...
Then seemingly back at the beginning—AGAIN.
This Wombman has known great happiness,
as well as deep dark sorrow that threatened to never end!
Confusing, startling New Beginnings with No Instructions,
No Manual! No how to fix it chart!
Juss another Start/A Broken Heart/Weary Feet/
And a Soul & Mind that wanted to eat!

I See that One within the mirror
With Moor Clarity & Purpose than I ever have!
And I Honor her in ways
that I did not Know to do before.
This New State of Knowing leads me to make a Self Decree:

I promise to Honor Myself more today than
I did yesterday by be-ing True to me at All times.

I promise to place no one else's opinions, Above my Own.
That the opinions/advice/musings of others are weighed
to see if it matches the person I AM today;
Or is it a better match for the person I used to be.
Or is it their stuff that they're trying to put on me(?!)

I Honor myself with Confidence that whatever
I need to Know, will Always come to me--Effortlessly
And I don't have to worry about the
Unknowns/Maybes/What-ifs!

I Honor Myself with Peace of Mind,
As my normal state of be-ing
that worry/anxiety/restlessness have been
evicted from their deep-seated-presence,
in my life, thoughts, emotions.

I Honor Myself with Deep Cleansing Breaths
signaling to the body temple, that I
have let go of the madness--
people/places/things that I have no control of
and today I accept that I never did.

I Honor Myself with better nutrition, adequate rest,
lots of water and yoga.

I Honor Myself by choosing wisely,
 those I Allow in my inner circle.

I Honor Myself with Good Music, Dance, and Pleasure.
I Honor Myself with inner and outer Beauty.
I Honor Myself with Time for Me:
Time to think w/o interruptions/outward chatter.
Time to consider, where I Am in my own process.
Time to be At-One-Ment w/ myself.
Time to do Absolutely Nothing~

I Honor Myself by be-ing Grounded/Rooted in the
Spiritual Teachings, Philosophies of Life
and Meditations, that feel right and make sense to me.

I Honor Myself by Opening my Heart Chakrah
Wider, that I May Give & Receive Love Much Deeper.

I Honor Myself by Respecting the rights of others
to make their own choices/live their lives in the
way it makes sense to them-Even if I disagree.

I Honor Myself with Lots of Belly-laughs! tears of Joy!
Good times and a host of Wonderfully New Adventures!

I Honor Myself with Gratitude for be-ing Alive & Well!

I Honor Myself through Creative Expression --
I go Deeper into this Craft/Artistry /expression of life
that Chose Me.
K. Mhina Entrantt© 2009

Emotional Home

Emotions are the postal services to your immune system. Emotions are what keep us honest, alert, and current, when we allow them to do what they were designed to do. You get a phone call, no matter who it is on the other line and what they say, your emotional system will *immediately* begin to give you a direct message: this is great! this is awful! this doesn't matter...this is surprising/unexpected! I hate this!

Emotions often get a bad rep and are often referred to as too much or not enough or good/bad/inappropriate. Emotions are none of these descriptors, emotions just ARE. Emotions are messengers, how we respond to the message is entirely up to us. Regardless if it's unexpected or something we don't like, the response is Always ours to choose. Yes, there are social graces and even laws which dictate the parameters or boundaries of how to/how not to respond and it still is a Choice to heed or not.

The purpose of emotions, are to get our attention that we may take this new information/data/revelation/un-folding through our personal code, memory, and previous choices to determine what the next step could be. When emotions are continuously ignored, minimalized, dismissed, maximized, used to hurt ourselves or others, or used as a crutch to remain stuck in old patterns, the body-temple home is greatly impacted and the need for medical attention will arise, if the purpose of emotions is not honored and adhered to.

For example: A close friend/family member whom you trust, asks, how you are doing, as you are dealing with a new break-up. Your verbal response: "oh I'm fine, I don't think about him/her at all." Your emotional response: your stomach begins to twist, your voice shakes—just a little and your eyes tear up…What are your emotional messages saying?-- I need comfort/I need solitude/I need to talk about how difficult this is for me right now. What will you do? Why?

> These Hands of Mine
> Lollipops, cookies, dirt, dolls, sandwiches.
> Books, papers, pencils, pens, homework.
> Amusement rides, beaches, parks, museums.
> Grade school, middle school, high school, college.
> Degrees, employment, taxes, lay-offs.
> Houses, dorms, apartments, rooms.
> Laughter, tears, wonder, relief.
> Joy, surprise, disappointment, release.
> My hands have touched them all!
> K. Mhina Entrantt, © 2009

Community Home

The spirit of a community comes forth when the soul of one connects with the soul of another. In other words, *like attracts like*. There is a *familial recognition and response*, although this may actually be a first time meeting. There's a light, warming feeling in the air, almost like an invisible sigh of relief. A natural conversation emerges and there is no need for filters and masks. Everything within and without, *feels* this state of *Alignment and Peace.* Without saying a word, there is a deep knowing, I AM Home~

The unfolding of Community Home occurs when, an intentional gathering of people willingly, effortlessly share Common Purpose/Ideas/ Information and Life Views; to connect by physical contact/words said/ or written or through emotional thoughts; to be in accord, at-one-ment, in fellowship with those of kindred spirits and aspirations. *Commune. Partnership. Harmony. Intimate association. Rapport. Sharing.*

Being at home in your Community is a heart-centered way of life. To purposely build relationships with those with whom you can be yourself, *as you are in the Now.* Often friendships, relationships and sometimes associations fall apart, lose connection with one another because the people have grown apart in some way. The "party gurle" of high school or college may choose a different path as she matures or becomes exposed to a different world. If her bonding relationships were primarily centered around the good-time-party-days, there will be a disconnect in those relationships. She may not be able to explain herself, why she has lost interest in activities she once enjoyed and participated in with high enthusiasm.

Many times the Ego is driving the bus when it comes to who we choose or attract into our world/circumstances. The choices are generally made out of fear, need for acceptance or validation, status symbol, or some form of distraction. Not all gatherings are communities, despite close physical proximity or surface similar interests. The Community Home comes without fanfare and fuss. Only heart invitations speak the language of community and we all feel the kinship of home.

What does Community look like?

When I was a child coming up I was surrounded by community in layers—one beside or on top of the other…everywhere I looked was a picture of community. There was Mrs. Holly who lived next door to my Godmother Babe, she raised funds to take the neighborhood children on bus trips throughout the summer. Somehow she was able to get buses, snacks, and drivers to arrive at her door to take all the children of at least 10 blocks of the neighborhood on field trips. Our parents paid a small amount of money for us to go on trips, which usually lasted the entire day. We were safe, we were supervised by adults from our neighborhood and we had a good time. We all knew one another, went to school together or to the same churches/temples. Just think how Mrs. Holly's labour of love kept the community strong, vibrant, and united. Parents who worked, during the summer months, didn't have to coordinate schedules with daycare/babysitters during trip days. Parents who were off, had a chance to have a breather, spend some quality time at home; couples may have had an afternoon delight without children in the home; teens were able to have activities to occupy their mind and time; younger children sat next to their friends and classmates as we rode in the large yellow school buses on our way to amusement parks, museums, cultural centers, zoos, exhibits, etc. *Children had a chance to just be children*—to run and play and laugh and explore and learn. The entire experience was enjoyable!

Mrs. Holly was a *Pillar of the community*. She had no agency or religious affiliation. She never ran for political office. She had one adult son and no grandchildren that I can recall. She was over 6' tall and 300 lbs. with long silver hair, that looked the same colour as the moon on a starry night. She usually pulled it back in a ponytail braid. She was brown like an oatmeal cookie, with long arms that the fatty part hung down when she moved them. As a child, I thought that meant she was really strong. She had a distinct voice, like someone who could have been a great orator. She was pretty in an ordinary-kind-of-way. What I loved most about Mrs. Holly was the bright summer colours she wore when we went on our trips. Most of the adults I knew rarely wore fashions or colours like that. Everything about Mrs. Holly said we were going to have fun! *Mrs. Holly gave of herself to the community for 3 generation of children.*

I was 3 ½ years old when my younger sister was born on a cold January day in the early 60's. When my mother returned home from the hospital, she and the baby remained upstairs in the bedroom for what seemed like a long time. I remember "Mother Walley" coming to our house, early in the morning to take care of my mother and the new baby. Mother Walley cooked breakfast for us and took breakfast up to my mother in bed. She cleaned the house, did the laundry, and prepared dinner before she left that afternoon. When my father arrived home from work that evening, the house was pristine, we were all taken care of and there was a warm meal on the stove.

Mother Walley was the persona of divine love, she was a quiet unassuming woman who just went her way spreading love and joy wherever she went. She was a medium size woman, with skin the beautiful colour of polished walnuts. She too had been a days worker and now she was retired. She had raised 11 children and had many grands and great-grands. She spent her days doing the practical, hands-on things, to help those in need. Mother Walley came to our house every other day until my mother was able to take care of the house again. On the days that Mother Walley didn't come, other women from the church came and did the same thing she had done. She refused to take any money for her contributions to others. She saw it as her assignment to the community. *Mother Walley was a visual for my young eyes to capture what a loving supportive community looks like on a daily basis.*

When I was a teen, my mother had a friend, Mrs. Sara who was very concerned about a young woman in her neighborhood who was a heroin addict with newborn twins. She often went to check on the woman and take care of the babies. My mother's friend tried to encourage the woman to go into treatment so these children would not have to be taken by the state as her other children had been. The woman agreed to go into treatment if Mrs. Sara would keep the babies, which she did. The young woman did not go into treatment, but went on a bender and stayed gone for about a month. When she showed back up, she was in worse condition than before. This back and forth dance went on for awhile, until it was clear the young woman's addiction was severe.

Mrs. Sara was so moved with compassion for the twins that she and her husband adopted the twins and raised them along with their other 9 children! They had an open adoption and every now and then the twins' mother would show up at Mrs. Sara's house to see the children. I was often there when their mother would suddenly show up, usually in disarray, hungry, and looking for money. Mrs. Sara always treated the woman with kindness. She fed her, tried to counsel her and encouraged her to get help for her addiction; however she did not give the woman money.

The twins had the opportunity to grow up in a loving, nurturing home with stable parents and lots of sisters and brothers. They became star scholars and athletes. They went on to lead very successful lives, *as the result of a concerned neighbor in their community making a choice to fulfill the needs of 2 little babies.*

A few years ago on a stormy Autumn Day I was on the bus, glad to be on my way home after a long work day. The bus was crowded with men and women from every walk of life and creed, who seemed to have the same mood of looking forward to being home soon. The bus route had changed and we were going down an unfamiliar street. As we got to the bus stop and the bus driver opened the doors, a man asked the driver if he was going to a specific location. The driver replied that he was not going that way. The man seemed anxious and begin to explain, he was standing there with a child who was lost and he did not know what to do to get the child to his destination.

At that moment you could feel the whole energy of the bus change—we were all listening intently. That lost child had in that instant became *our child.* The bus driver told the child to get on the bus and he would see to it that he got home, if he had to drive the bus to his home, personally. A soaking wet-crying 11 year old White male child began to step on the bus. He was so scared about getting lost he was crying and could not catch his breath as he entered the bus, shaking like a lost scared puppy.

People began to scoot over to make room for him to sit in the front of the bus. A very tall Black woman walked over to him, guided him to a seat, took off her full length leather coat and wrapped it around him; a Jewish woman begin to talk to him and gave him her phone to call home; the bus driver called home base to report a lost child; the people in the office also begin to try to reach the child's parents; An older woman took her scarf off and wiped his face and dried his soaking-wet-new-haircut; A Latino man gave him a sandwich to eat; A Black man handed him money; An Asian woman gave him candy and I talked reassuringly to him and gave him water to drink. We all pitched in effortlessly. We forgot how tired we all were and how much we just wanted to get home. Not one person complained or said one disturbing word. *We became a safe, comforting community for a lost, scared child.*

When he could catch his breath he began to tell us how he had gone to his friend's house after school to play a video game. He was having such a good time he lost track of time. When he realized he should go before his parents got home and found out he had not went straight home from school, he got his backpack and left. It was now dark and he became confused, he had been walking in the cold rain for over 2 hours. He did not have a jacket with him because it was not cold when he left school. Someone behind him put their hand on his shoulder.

He sat eating his sandwich, putting money in his pocket, and drinking a sip of water. After he finished eating the sandwich, he put a piece of candy in his mouth. Whenever someone reached their stop, before they got off the bus they would stand in front of the lost child and assure him he was safe and he was going to be alright. He looked up at the person with the most beautiful eyes, as though he was thinking, because you say I am safe and I will be alright, I will believe it.

I got off the bus before the child reached his destination, but I knew he was in good hands, the community had arose to the call, to protect and help one of the lost young ones. I often wondered about the imprint that experience left on the heart and mind of that young child… who he may become or what path he may later choose as a result of such a personal experience with this demonstration of community.

This was community in its finest hour on a Seattle bus on a cold, blustering rainy Autumn Day in 2010.

The If-Response From Your Neighborhood!?

If we had known your house was such an unhappy place for a child…

We would've made sure our houses were open, for you to come to,

whenever you needed to get away from the chaos.

If we had paid attention and realized

your lil innocence was in danger…or had been

touched…taken…and stolen away…

We would've done whatever was necessary

 to protect you and make the violence…

the betrayal…the devastation stop!

If we had taken the time to see,

jus how broken you were from the inside out…

We would've stepped in earlier, to help mend the broken pieces,

put them back together and we would've

stayed around til the healing was complete!

If we had had the foresight/vision, to see how

 alcohol, crack, meth, heroin and all the others, would destroy our neighborhoods….

We would've united and kept it away from you…

away from your mom…

away from your granny…

away from your dad…

away from your auntie…

away from sis…

away from bro…

away from you!

If we had sensed, your need for

 more love…

more attention…

more time…

more support…

more of us, in your life…

No matter what, we would've made time for you…

we would've told you that you mattered…

we would've shown you daily,

jus how much we love and care for you!

If we had realized your destiny for greatness was in jeopardy,

because your pain was so great, your hurts had been too many,

and your hope for a better life had died a long time ago;

We would've provided shelter, nurtured, and nourished you

with the best that we had to give.

We would've invested our time, our money, our words, into your young life.

We would've paved a smoother road for you to walk on

and been your bridge to success.

If we had known jus how bad you needed someone,

anyone checking on you and checking in with you;

We would've have done that, effortlessly, for you were ours too.

So today, all these years later we take the time to apologize...

to bow our heads in sorrow...

to bend our knees,

as tears roll down our faces...

for we now see what our lack of participation has cost us all....

We acknowledge and accept the responsibility as your neighborhood,

we dropped the ball...we allowed your precious lil life

to fall between the cracks...

we turned our heads when we could've held out our hands...

we too were a part of the problem...

instead of being a part of the solution!

Today, we deeply regret that!

Know for sure, If we had known better,

we would've done better

by you and for you!

Signed, your neighborhood~

K. Mhina Entrantt ©2011

Money Home

Where does your money reside/live/dwell? When you think of money is it in context of what you don't have/won't have/ and can't have? When you think of your deepest desires are your first thoughts on how impossible it is because you don't have enough money? Are you afraid of money? Do you think you would lose your family, friends, quality of life, as a result of having abundance of money? Are you blocked by subtle thoughts about having an abundance of money = lack of spirituality/morals?

What is faith? It is the confident assurance that something we want is going to happen. It is the certainty that what we hope for is waiting for us, even though we cannot see it up ahead.

Hebrews 11:1, Living Bible

Now faith is being sure of what we hope for and certain of what we do not see. This is what the ancients were commended for.

Hebrews 11:1-2, New International Bible

Now faith is the substance of things hoped for, the evidence of things not seen. For by it the elders obtained a good report.

Hebrews 11:1-2, King James Bible

There is no problem in any situation that faith will not solve. There is no shift in any aspect of the problem but will make solution impossible. For if you shift part of the problem elsewhere the meaning of the problem must be lost, and the solution to the problem is inherent in its meaning. Is it not possible that all your problems have been solved, but you removed yourself from the solution? Yet faith must be where something has been done, and where you see it done.

A Course In Miracles Chapter 17, VII, 2 (1 – 4)

In any situation in which you are uncertain, the first thing to consider, very simply is "What do I want to come of this? What is it for? The clarification of the goal belongs at the beginning, for it is this which will determine the outcome. In the ego's procedure this is reversed. The situation becomes the determiner of the outcome, which can be anything. The ego does not know what it wants to come of a situation. It is aware of what it does not want, but only that. It has no positive goal at all. Without a clear cut positive goal set at the outset, the situation just seems to happen and makes no sense until it has already happened. Then you look back at it, and try to piece together what it must have meant. And you will be wrong. Not only is your judgment in the past. But you have no idea what should happen. No goal was set with which to bring the means in line. And now the only judgment left to make is whether the ego likes it; is it acceptable; or does it call for revenge? The absence of criterion for outcome set in advance, makes understanding doubtful and evaluation impossible.

The value of deciding in advance what you want to happen is simply that you will perceive the situation as a means to make it happen. You will therefore make every effort to overlook what interferes with the accomplishment and concentrate on everything that helps you meet it.

A Course In Miracles Chapter 17, VI, 2 - 4

When they came to Capernaum, the collectors of the half shekel tax went up to Peter and said, "does not your teacher pay the tax? He said "Yes." When he came home, Jesus spoke to him first…go to the sea and cast a hook, and take the first fish that comes up and when you open his mouth you will find a *shekel, (*See The History of Money.) *take that and give it to them for me and yourself.*

Matthew 17: 24-27, Revised Standard Bible

There is no order of difficulty in miracles. One is not harder or bigger than another. They are all the same. All expressions of love are maximal.

A Course In Miracles Chapter 1, I, 1 (1-4)

Miracles are natural. When they do not occur something has gone wrong.

A Course In Miracles Chapter 1, I, 6

A miracle is a correction introduced into false thinking by me. It acts as a catalyst, breaking up erroneous perception and reorganizing it properly. This places you under the Atonement principle, where perception is healed. Until this has occurred, knowledge of the Divine Order is impossible.

A Course In Miracles Chapter 1, I, 37 (1-4)

We are convinced that under Divine Law all things are possible, if we only believe and work in conformity with the principles of that Law. Such a faith does not spring full-orbed into being; but grows by knowledge and experience. No matter what the outside appearance, we must cling steadfastly to the knowledge that God is good and God is all, underneath, above, and round about.

The Science of Mind, Earnest Holmes

Life is nothing less than a creative force, an act of becoming rather than a static state of being. Everything you do from the first breath you take, is a part of the process of creation. Yet we often hold on to and crystallize emotions, events, and things. Change or evolution makes us feel out of control, so we resist. Resistance brings tension and stress. Change inevitably does come, only now it's through crisis. If we can learn to go with the flow, to trust ourselves and have faith that life is not just chaos and happenstance, that there is meaning and reason for everything that happens to us, and that we are part of that meaning and reason, then we can meet both the challenges and triumphs without losing our purpose, our identity, or our centeredness.

Linda Joyce, The Day You were Born

Faith is centered in, and cooperates with, Divine Mind. Because we fail to realize that Principle is not bound by precedent, we limit our faith to that which has already accomplished and few "miracles" result. When, through intuition, faith finds its proper place under Divine Law, there are no limitations, and what are called miraculous results follow.

The Science of Mind, Earnest Holmes

Money is *Currency*.

The original meaning for *Currency* is: *in circulation, having movement, no stagnation*. *Currency* is closely linked to the words *Cycle* and *Circle*, depicting continuous movement and flow. This goes back to the ancient days of sacred math and shapes. The Egyptians, Mayans, Buddhist, and many other tribal nations adhered to the laws of the sacred math and shapes and saw it as evidence that all living forms are in union with one another and inter-dependent—what happens with one life form, impacts another. The ancients knew how important it was to keep the flow going and *to go with the flow. The cycle/circle of life was always in the currency, flowing infinitely upon all*

The definition of money as we *conceptualize* it today was expanded, when paper money became the *medium of exchange* for goods and services. Money as we know it today has not always existed. It is almost unfathomable that, there was a time when paper and coin money was not the medium of exchange for goods and services. How *Current* is your money?

Our ancestors had a completely different system and in many areas that economic system did not change until the 20th century. They made their business arrangements according to what was available in their environments and what they needed from other areas. This was how they determined their own medium of exchanges; certain shells, beads, crops, etc. were highly valued and was the medium of exchange for goods and services. In some remote areas today, paper money has no value or place in their exchanges with others. A million dollars means nothing in their world!

We have been socially conditioned to give All our power to money. In our minds, money has become synonymous with the ability to obtain what we truly desire. The dollar amount has been given the sole power of determining what we can and can't have. We have been lured into the realm of hard work actions, being the only way to get what we want. This belief system is what causes people to work in jobs they hate, stay in careers they are no longer passionate about and return home depleted in body/mind/spirit, daily. Yet, it seems the harder you work, the less gets accomplished and the further away your deepest hopes and dreams become… primarily, because money is in control of your life. You have subconsciously allowed money to become your master and you the servant. This is how and why the feasibility of the Law of Attraction is not possible for most people. The social conditioning and belief that

*the only pathway, of having what you truly want and desire happening-- is through hard work--
is so ingrained, such a well-substantiated pillar in their minds...it is all they can accept~*

K. Mhina Entrantt

What type of energy does your money live in? What are your most fluent thoughts about money on a daily basis? Is your money energy surrounded by all the examples of what doesn't work? What failed? What was lost? What was *not* available to you in childhood because of the *lack* of money?

If, money was a person and you could have a sit down conversation with this entity, how would you spend your time with money? Would you fuss and cuss at money for all the times you feel money let you down or would you acknowledge in the past you did not know how to have a good relationship with money and you're willing to learn now—can you help me? Would you talk to money as a beggar pleading for crumbs of bread off the King/Queen's table? Or would you name all the people in your circle of family and friends who have *never* fared well because they didn't/don't have money and that was unfair and you are angry/hurt/sad...about that?

Are you nervous/anxious/hyper-viligilent/care-free/resourceful/short-sighted/in-experienced/capable/needing help/uncertain/at ease/depleted/sufficient/ample abundant/prosperous/increasing/ balanced/in-harmony—about your Money(?!)

The History of Money

During ancient times, money was a type of receipt which represented the amount of grain stored in temple storehouses. Many cultures around the world eventually developed the use of commodity money. *The shekel was originally a unit of weight, and referred to a specific weight of barley, which was used as currency. In Asia, Africa and Australia shell money was the currency.

The shells of cowries were used for centuries as currency throughout Africa. Ghanaian currency known as the *Ghanaian cedi* was named after cowrie shells. In Western Africa, shell money was used until almost the 20th century. Cowrie shells, sometimes spelled *cowry*, come from small to large sea snails. These snails are in the same family as mussels, slugs, and clams. The shells have translucent-like features, have similar shapes to an egg except for flatness on the underside, and vary in size. Cowrie shells were easy to handle and pleasant to look at. The shells were used in many remote parts of Africa, which were not easily accessed by outside countries, until the early 20th century.

Cowrie shell money was called *nzimbu*. The *value* of the cowrie shells was very high in West Africa and the trade was extremely lucrative. Sometimes the increase was as much as 500%. The use of the cowrie currency gradually spread inland in Africa. In the countries on the coast, the shells were fastened together in strings of 40 or 100 each, so that fifty or twenty strings represented a dollar; but in the interior they were counted one by one, or five by five. They were known as *kurdi* to some and *simbi* to others.

In Benguella, Portuguese West Africa, the shell of the large land snail was cut into circles with an open center was also used as coin. It was almost the 21st century before the majority changed their *currency systems* to the manner of the modern *medium of money*.

The ancient tribes of the Ojibway Aboriginees in North America used cowrie shells for trade and ceremonies. According to the birch bark scrolls the shells were found in the ground, or washed up on the shores of rivers. It is believed this use of the cowrie shells for currency goes back at least 10,000 years or more. The Whiteshell Provincial Park in Manitoba, Canada is named after the cowrie shell.

In the Fiji Islands, a shell of the golden cowrie is worn on a string around the neck of chieftains as a badge of honor, prestige, and status.

The shell most valued by the Native American tribes of the Pacific Coast from Alaska to Northwest California was Dentalium shell, a long narrow marine shelled mollusk, a tusk shell or scaphopod. The tusk shell had openings at both ends, which made it much easier to string with a thread. The shell money was valued by length rather than the number of shells; the "ligua" was the highest denomination of currency, it was a length of 6 feet.

Native Americans in Southern California, used the shell from the olive snail as currency. The Iroquois, Algonquian, Shinnecock Tribes ground beads cut from the purple part of the shell of the hard clam. The beads were called *wampum* and were used for adorning and trading.

In the early American colonies, money was not available and other forms of exchange *took on the same value as money*. Such things as beaver fur and wampum were used as money in the north for exchanges with the Indians, and fish and corn also served as money. In South Carolina rice was the money exchange.

The most valuable exchange in the place of money in the South was tobacco, esp. in Virginia. A pound of tobacco served as the currency in Virginia. Warehouse receipts in tobacco *circulated as money* backed 100 percent by the tobacco in the warehouse. This is the same system as the ancients used, just refreshed by changing the medium of the exchange.

In northern Australia, different shells were used by different tribes, one tribe's shell value did not always hold the same value for another tribe. They devised mediums of exchange which were acceptable to one another.

In China Cowrie shell money was used from the 16th – 8th century. The Classical Chinese character for money or currency was a symbol of a cowrie shells. Over three thousand years ago, cowry shells and copies of the shells, were used as Chinese currency.

According to historians, the Classical Chinese character for *money*(貝) originated as a stylized drawing of a Maldivian cowrie shell. Words and characters concerning money, property or wealth usually have this as a radical. Before the Spring and Autumn period the cowrie was used as an type of trade token awarding access to a feudal lord's resources to a worthy vassal. They were also used as means of exchange in India.

Cowrie shell money was also used in India, Thailand. Other examples of commodities that have been used as mediums of exchange include gold, silver, copper, salt, peppercorns, large stones (such as Rai stones), decorated belts, shells, alcohol, cigarettes, cannabis, candy, and barley. These items were sometimes used in a metric of perceived value in conjunction to one another, in various commodity values.

This brief look at the history of money clearly shows that, those doing the exchanges determined the value of whatever medium of exchange they agreed to use for the circulation of goods and services. Today that determination is made by the governing body of a specific country that determines the acceptable medium for the exchange of goods and services. The determination of the value of the medium of exchange is also determined by the governing body of the country.

As we look back at the original history of money, we learn actual paper money as we know it today, is not always necessary for the medium of exchange for goods and services. Agreements for exchanges of services, products, information, and transportation may still be reached. When Person Y has the goods or services, which Person X sees as valuable, necessary, and Person X has goods and services that Person Y sees as desirable, valuable, necessary; and mutual mediums of exchanges can be agreed upon, the attainment of good and services is possible.

For example you are unemployed and can no longer afford to get your grass cut. Your neighbor loves to do yard work. As the both of you are talking one morning, he talks about how he and his wife would give anything to have a date night but can't fit a babysitter in their budget yet. *What non-monetary-exchange could happen that would be beneficial and have mutual value for you and your neighbor?*

My maternal grandfather was born in 1900, he was the son of a Cherokee mother and a Black father. He was the colour of roasted walnuts. He was a Shaman, Healer, Griot. I found him to be an interesting man and I loved to hear his stories. My grandfather was a very prayerful man. He had certain times of the month when he would "fast and pray." This meant he would not eat or drink *anything* for at least *40 days*. He did all the activities of his usual routine, including working a very physical job on the docks for as long as I can remember. If someone in the family became ill, he immediately went into his *consecration time*—he would pray for the person's recovery and not eat or drink until the recovery was complete.

I've known him to go for as long as 3 months or more without food or drink. It was common in our family to talk about healings from brain cancer, heart attacks, paralysis, tumors, blood disorders, individuals coming out of comas and the like, because of Grandpop's prayers. Whenever someone went into the hospital and the doctor said they wouldn't make it through the night—a call was made to my grandfather who went to the hospital, laid hands on the person and sat with the person through the night saying affirmative prayers about the body being restored. Every person my grandfather prayed for was restored to optimum health!

It was fascinating to me to actually talk to someone who had lived through the history I was studying in school! I remember in 9th grade I had an assignment to research about the Great Depression and write an essay. Rather than look through a bunch of dusty books, I decided to *interview Grandpop*. It was the early 70's and I was very interested to hear how Black people made it through such a challenging economic time.

Grandpop described to me in great detail how he worked 2 and 3 jobs per day, walking from one end of town to the complete opposite and back again to provide enough food each day for his large family. He told how most of the "day jobs" were extremely heavy labor and only lasted 2 – 3 hours. He said there was no distance that he was not willing to walk to get to the next job. He left his house before dawn and sometimes did not get back home until after 10 pm. He always came home with enough money for food and the absolute essentials. Grandpop described for hours how he and his family were able to meet their needs on a daily basis until the economy turned around. During those lean days Grandpop kept his home, the children were fed and cared for and he never loss faith. He *expected* to get through those challenging times and he did!

The Smell of Life

Life is like a pot of soup.
First you start with a good size pot.
Then you add your water, but not too much.
Next is the heat. All good soups have to have enough
heat to cause a boiling.
Then comes the seasonings—and that's always to your own taste.
Some folks call this the taste of life. Then comes the veggies—with
their different colors, textures, tastes; choices, decisions, and
experiences. All coming in at the same time!
Then comes the meat also known as the core of life's lessons and
principles.
Now it's time for the stirring.

The funny thing about stirrings is they can look like trouble, conflict, pain and other stuff that you don't want.
You need a nice long handle to stir it just right—you know those times when the right somebody shows up to give you just what you needed that day..!
After all that good stirring, the soup begins to blend and give off its own aroma.
Who could've known that a stirring would give off such a pleasant fragrance?
Now it's time to go get your earthen vessel and pour you some soup. Doesn't that feel so warm... so good... so tasty going down?
K. Mhina Entrantt © 2009

Initiation III: The Connection of Zebra Medicine

Passion Home

Courage Home

Trust Home

The Lessons, Symbols and Alchemy of Zebra Stripes are about the union of opposites, the balance of instinct and intuition, the energy of yin and yang, Shakti and Shiva. These lessons and principles help us to realize in life, there can be differences, balance, and harmony, all at the same time. Zebra Medicine shows us how we can have a cohesive community and still be an individual. As we mature and expand, we realize nothing is really just black or white; there are always gray areas. What is an absolute for you, may not be plausible for someone else; the other person may have a totally different *perspective*. This doesn't necessarily make either person wrong/a liar/ or stupid, the angle of the view is different. Zebra stripes teach us how to find common ground in every situation. The questions become: *How can I show you respect and not give my own power away? Where can we meet and agree, without anyone feeling disrespected/compromised? How can we still work together in harmony instead of resentment?*

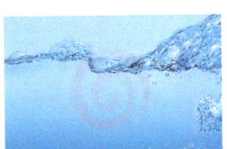

"Reason is the offspring of thought…"
Tjeuti, Original Father of Medicine, Ancient Egyptian Sage

The Lessons of Zebra Medicine begin to awaken some time, between the 4th and 5th decade of physical life. It is the deep initiation of the Great Mother-Feminine Principle, where the willingness to embrace Passion, Courage, and Trust begin to emerge. The seamless union of the divine and hue-man transformations are now possible! This is the state of Be-ing-ness where One begins to stand on their own feet, identifies with soul-purpose; while simultaneously uniting with one's larger community and contributing as needed.

We have the capacity to continue to live/grow/expand, perpetually. Modern culture often focuses on youth and pop culture.

The messages of life being over/going downhill after the ages of 30/40/50/60+ are so prevalent that we can be convinced not to look for life to be full of Passion, Abundance, and Prosperity.

In Cultures that do not have rituals, customs, or observances of life passages; the lessons of Zebra Medicine-- this ancient jewel, is often missed/overlooked/disregarded.

According to our Ancient Egyptian Sages, the body is programmed to automatically go through a Biological Regeneration on a regular basis; the physical body has the capacity to totally renew itself every 7 years and there are other renewals taking place throughout all the systems of the body in less than 7 years, such as all soft tissue systems in the body go through a revitalization process every 7 months. This was considered one of the *Secrets for Mastering the Physical Body*.

The animal kingdom can teach us so many things, if we are willing to open our eyes and hearts. As long as there is life within and without there is still more to learn and do.

The mind needs new information, stimulation, projects to think through and work on. It too must stay agile to function at its capacity. Modern day research says we rarely use more than 10% of our mental capacity. Just imagine the possibilities, if we decided to go further than 10%!

Each zebra has its own stripe pattern, similar to human fingerprints or DNA—no 2 zebras are exactly alike. Native Americans and other ancient cultures depict zebras as the symbol for seeing in black and white, having the ability to be an individual and support community, balance, clarity, sure-footing, and agility. When we open ourselves up to what the Zebras have to teach us, we too can learn the art and practice of being a secure individual who is also capable of uplifting the community.

The joining of the Zebras is what keeps them safe and protected in the safari. As a group their patterns of stripes are too confusing for predators to easily attack; their keen senses and ability to move quickly are tools they use often. There are times when we must be alert and aware and know when it is time to move or leave the area because it no longer provides sustenance, figuratively or literally. Studying zebras and how they live and survive could be more useful than you could possibly imagine.

Zebras are known to be nomads on a quest to the next adventure, looking for new resources of sustenance. Zebras stay alert and adjust to changes as needed, quickly. Zebras are quick on their feet, have panoramic vision, excellent memory, and have clear vision of the what and why. If, it is time to find a new source of food and water, they go forward until they have obtained the vision. They stay focused until the goal is completed.

Zebras require lots of water and must share the water source with their predator, the lion. The animal kingdom has found a way for opposites to live in the same area, eat off the land, and drink from the same water source. Can we become good stewards over the life lessons they can teach us, if we are aware? This is the Initiation of the Houses of Passion, Courage, and Trust.

Passion Home!

There is A seed... A spark... A knowing... A voice...within us all! It is of and from the divine. Every baby comes here with "it." Although we may have unknowingly disconnected from our Passion it never fully goes away, we can call it back through self- integrity and joy.   K. Mhina Entrantt

Passion is the salivation of the soul. It is the internal flame of joy, freedom, forgiveness, acceptance, expansion, and healthy satisfying relationships. It lays dormant within the core of a person, until the appropriate stirring brings it forth. Passion is to the soul what the spinal cord is to the physical body. *Without Passion, it is impossible to lead a completely fulfilling, satisfying life!* Life may still be good, one may be able to contribute wonderful things to the community, and finances may not be an issue. Yet, there is the stench of decay in some part of one's life, when Passion is dead/dying/stuck. Stagnation brings death to new ideas, new resources, new friends and family, new projects, new money streams, new hopes and dreams. There is a block in the 4th Chakrah and it will show up in the physical and emotional bodies, if Passion is not resuscitated. Passion is the life-force of the body/mind/spirit.

The birthing canal of Passion is as crushing of grapes for wine, stomping of olives for virgin olive oil, or the hidden dampness of an unbridled coal which holds the diamond in place until qualifying heat releases it.

Passion is the collaboration of the essence of the person and the fullness of the divine. It is the song you hum as you fix their favorite meal; it is the electronic card via email; it is the *I love you* text; it is the FB check in; it is the smile for your child's first steps; it is the encouraging pat on the back; it is the creative lesson plan; it is the apology given and accepted; it is honoring the end of a relationship and the openness for a new one; it is the backdrop for a painter's brush and empty pages, just waiting for the writer's ink; it is the gathering of friends and family; it is a comforting hand reaching out to one in need. *It is the divine in physical form.* It is the Absolute Y-O-U, seeping onto the pages of your life and the lives of others.

To rightfully handle Passion, one must successfully return home after the quest, rise from the ashes of disappointments, fear, anger, un-forgiveness and blame; willingly breathe-in the breath of new life and go forward in harmony and balance.

Passion is an inner spark of light which flickers on when a divine idea, thought, creation, or action is allowed to come forth, to grow, to reach its' *Full* completion; free from the interruptions of fear, rejection, or minimalizing. Passion wakes you up in the middle of night with the hint of a new idea, new project, a new path of life. Passion is energetic, outrageous, humorous and life-changing! Passion makes your heart sing, puts an extra step/strut in your walk, and gives you the confidence to go forward—no matter what!

Courage Home

The Ancient Ones *created* the word Courage, for they exemplified it in their traditions, their belief systems, rituals, and every aspect of currency which they daily lived. It was natural, *to go with the flow*; to observe the elements of nature, animals, vegetation, seasons, rotation of the sun and planets. They were in-tuned to their environment and had the courage to follow the rhythm of nature. Scientists all over the world are still trying to figure out how the Dogon People of Mali were able to record intricate details of sun, stars, planets and the celestials on their walls for thousands of years and still do—no telescopes, no computers, no machinery, yet they have absolute precision in their tales of the celestials.

Courage is the willingness to stand in the strength of your own personal code of truth without the need for validation of others; the ability to live through your intuition and heart, rather than solely depending on the ego for guidance and instructions; the conviction to say/do/be, who you really are—*from the inside out and the ability to keep expanding*.

Although physical courage gets the most attention, there is so much more at stake when we begin to peel back the outward layers of courage. Absent of rites of passages, kinship communities, and honor for our Elders, it is challenging for modern day generations to grasp what courage truly is. The true essence of Courage is seamlessly tied to the 42 Principles of MAAT. It takes courage to walk the pathways of integrity, character, self-discipline, and honor for oneself and others, during an era when such intrinsic beliefs as "the end justifies the means;" "it's a dog-eat-dog-world;" "it's a rat race" are commonly accepted.

Contrary to popular opinion, peer pressure does not start in the teen years. Adults in every facet of life are regularly confronted by someone in their close circle, trying to persuade, cajole, or influence them to do something, which is outside of their personal code of behavior, business practices, ethics, spiritual beliefs or morals, "just this once…" It takes courage to walk away, speak up, or say no!

It takes Courage *not* to join the family business, because your passion is elsewhere. It takes Courage to move away, strike out on your own. It takes Courage not to marry the person someone else has type-cast for you. It takes Courage to end a mutually-unhealthy relationship. It takes Courage to know when to speak and to know when not to speak. It takes Courage to make a Decision and stick by it, when obstacles show up. It takes Courage to forgive and release old wounds. It takes Courage to allow your heart to open and love again. It takes Courage to get back up, after falling down. It takes Courage to apologize. It takes Courage to accept an apology. It takes Courage to listen to your body and rest. It takes Courage to embrace solitude. It takes Courage to make time for fun and relaxation. *It takes Courage to say Yes to life!*

To see what is right and not do it is want of courage.

Confucius

*Courage without conscience is a wild beast.*

Ralph Ingersoll

Trust Home

Trust is an inside-job! I cannot, will not, and do not trust the divine, if I do not trust myself! The trust I seek from others begins within me. K. Mhina Entrantt

The word *Trust* like the word *Love* has been so mistreated, dishonored, abused, used for gain, and manipulated that allowing or receiving Trust has morphed into a meaningless gesture or a facade in hopes of selfish and irresponsible gain. The use of the word *Trust* now days, is suspect unless it's regarding money exchanges or money supervision. The language and feelings of: "I trust you." "I trust what you say is truthful." I trust that you will do right by me." "I trust you with my heart;" sticks to our immune systems as well as, our physical and emotional bodies, esp. when it appears the *Trust* has been broken, disrespected, or damaged beyond repair. Although the relationship may have happened long ago; the people involved may even be deceased; you may have married/have a long term relationship with another—and yet right beneath the surface, there are scabs, scars, cuts, lacerations, wounds on the skin of your Trust.

The Principle of Trust begins in the farmer's garden, in the field, on the vine, within the trees. Before the farmer plants his seeds in the soil, he makes close observations of the soil, conditions, weather patterns of the area, sun rotation, etc. The farmer then uses the information he has gathered, to determine which seeds, crops, or trees are best suited for the area he has observed. *Although he may have an abundance of seeds, he takes the time to match the seeds with the soil.* He knows which seeds require lots of sun, as opposed to those that require less sun. He knows his harvest depends on knowing when and where to plant the seed.

Sometimes, painful things happened during our childhood and we made a decision to close down our *Trust Home*, Or our ability to discern who is trustworthy for a particular situation is lacking, Or immaturity in how to navigate and interact with others, leads us into downward spirals, which are challenging to overcome.

We often plant our *Seeds of Trust* in unknown soil, hardened soil, soil which hasn't had enough nutrients to bring forth life, or soil that is not well suited for the harvest we desire to reap and glean. Once committed to one of these soils, we stubbornly, immaturely, and un-wisely toil land, which will never produce what we desire. It is usually the roughness of the ground which forces us to eventually stop working so hard for something that will never happen. We walk away with our hearts and tools broken, discouraged, damaged. We focus on how hard we worked and how much effort we gave and feelings of rejection, confusion, and dejection surround us like a mushroom bomb and we fall to pieces, on the spot and rarely are able to gather all the pieces of ourselves back again.

Unfortunately, because we did not gain the insight and wisdom of what actually took place, we repeat this pattern infinitum and have some version of the same results each time.

Baby Girle,

Sit down

Take off ur too-high designer shoes.

Put ur Coach/designer x bag down.

Rub ur hurting feet.

pull them up, til the heels can feel the cushion in the chair.

Or Stretch them out on the coffee table–

I know it's beautiful/fav stuff on it

but juss thys once, push it aside,

Stretch ur feet out & close ur eyes!

And juss be still for a minute.

No music. No ipod. no x-box.

Juss u & ur long loss/neglected friend–

Silence!

No thoughts about ray-ray/nae/niqua/or the dude u really like;

but he don't know it!

Juss U & Silence.

Silence will guide u, 2

Go upstairs.

Take off all ur

Impressn-my-peopl-gear-so-that-can't-c-my-fears~

Pull ur hair back.

Wash all the make-up off ur face, body.

Run a hot bubble bath.

Like u used to do back n the day.

No fancy label, juss somethin w/ good bubbles.

Get in & juss submerge all of u

Into the mystery of lathering/soothin/bubbles...

U close ur eyes, surrendering 2 the comfort of the bubbles...

U seemed to have drifted between the wurlds...

U hear a soft soothin voice

 Baby Girle, there are many around u

who never died.

There's the Ancestral Governing Council

led by Mother Matriarche herself...

The Chief Elders & the Scrybes--

They are where u really came from,

that's ur tribe!

Scrybes choose to live a different life than most

Becuz they know the real deal--more than most!

Go back 2 letting Simplicity be ur guide also.

She can show u how to look good & not be almost nekit;

she can help u save $ cuz u don't have 2 buy the new

thing soon as it comes on the market.

She can remind u of ur own inner integrity & that u don't

have to compromise urself or ur values, juss so ur not alone

or juss so u can have a man hold you through the nite.

She'll remind u ,ur worthy of a man that'll be around

in the day-lite 2.

Ur house ain't on fire, u don't need a rescue.

In the Silence u will Always be guided what to do..next.

U'll see, u no longer have to sacrifice ur Self-esteem..for—you know what!

U Baby Girle are Worthy of the Best...

U wake up..feelin as though tyme has stood still...

And evry bubble is still in place...

Until u realize those aren't bubbles, but tears on ur face~

K. Mhina Entrantt © 2009

Out of fear, desperation, immaturity, and need for validation from others, we refuse to heed the voice of the internal Mother, when she warns us not to open the deepest door of our Trust Home to one who is yet unknown. If a tree is known by the fruit it bears, then surely, a person is known by their *pattern* of behaviors and will Not change, unless they choose to. The bank has a vault to store the largest amount of money, jewels, bank notes, safety deposit boxes and other items of great value. Even if the bank is robbed by numerous people, rarely are they able to *access the vault*. Security, protection, and guidelines are in place to make sure the most precious remains safe. During business hours the bank is open and customers have *limited access* within the bank. We would do well, to have the same guidelines in our lives, regarding our Trust Home.

Sometimes we erroneously give Trust, where we should have given observation, conversation, interaction, association, casual encounters. It is not impolite to take the time to weigh an option, question, inquiry, or proposition. It is not impolite or disrespectful to say no, let me think about that, let me get back to you, I don't know about that, I'm not sure. It is not impolite to say tell me more about that, what does that mean? That won't work for me.

When trust is immature or undeveloped, it is easy to confuse minimal conversation, perceived interest, inquiries, compliments and subtle flirtations with meaningful attraction, intimate relationship interest, or potential for something you desire to happen. In the wild, a baby animal will run towards danger or a predator because their *instincts* are not yet set. It is usually the Mother that will push them out of harm's way, growl or hiss at the predator to make sure it stays away. We have lost our way, silenced the inner and outer Voice of the Mother Principle and in so doing, do not know how to live in our Home of Trust.

The Principle of Trust is Sacred and is the initiation of the 7th Chakrah. Trust is of the Divine. It is of the highest level of Love and receiving. This depth of relationship is only meant to be enacted between the person and the divine.

Through social conditioning we have been erroneously herded into thinking and trying to have with others, the depth of relationship one can only have with the divine. Unconditional Trust in All can only exist with the Divine. For it is of the Divine to know you from your deepest essence, to nurture you down to the place where the marrow and bone meet, to willingly accept all of you, in every state. It is beyond human capacity to attain this Realm of

Trust in engaging, relating with one another. To insist on having this completion of trust within human relationships is an exercise in futility and perpetual disappointments. *Our ability to trust has become fragile because we thought we could have with one another, what was really meant to have with the divine.*

> *The seventh chakra is our connection to our spiritual nature and our capacity to allow our spirituality to become an integral part of our physical lives and guide us. While our energy system as a whole is animated by our spirit, the seventh chakra is directly aligned to seek an intimate relationship with the Divine. It is the chakra of prayer. It is also our "grace bank account," the warehouse for the energy we amass through kind thoughts and actions, and through acts of faith and prayer. The seventh chakra represents our connection to the transcendent dimension of life.*
>
> Caroline Myss, Anatomy of the Spirit

What is readily available in hue-man to hue-man relationships is the *Principle of Honorable Agreements*. It can be said this is the description of t-r-u-s-t…the word with a small t. These are the attributes:

- *A conscious decision, to deal with one another with respect, high esteem, and care.*
- *To be clear with one another as to the type of relationship, business or encounter you agree to engage in and what that looks like for each person and to refrain from hidden agendas.*
- *To respectfully re-visit the terms of agreement, if major points are no longer working or someone wishes to change the agreement.*
- *To willingly talk with one another and address conflicts as they arise.*
- *To agree to disagree, sometimes and still be able to find common ground.*
- *To acknowledge the natural ebbs and flows of the relationship, business, encounters.*
- *To grant one another, if necessary, the freedom of ending what no longer works in dignity and grace.*

Hey Baby, I want to say thank you!

I thank you for expressing and sharing your private, deep thoughts with me today!

Because my thoughts were so off the mark from yours and I would've responded in the absolute wrong way—

And may have caused you to shut down or at best, close an emotional door with me!

As I saw you in deep thought and so wanted to ask you, were you ok?

I could not ask the question because I thought your dark mood had something to do with me(?!)

So I went into my head of "maybes"…maybe you've grown tired of this thing we have and you jus don't know how to tell me…

Maybe you've allowed another to discover what we do in our private under cover…

Maybe you're sick unto death and you're getting your things together…so I'll be ok when you're gone(?!)

As you can see, we won't do well, if we aren't grown enough to have our own show and tell.

Most of the time you put on such a façade of strong-black-man-holding-it-down-doin-fine!

That it never occurred to me, that the thing I considered just a bump in the road was a painful failure to you~

I knew daddy was sick, but I always expected him to get well.

You held your emotions so tight; I would've never known that you weren't alright.

I want to let you know that you don't have to be strong-all-the=time to have my love,

jus do what you did today, express yourself!

K. Mhina Entrantt© 2009

If the attributes of Honorable Agreement have never been discussed and agreed to by all, minimally glazed over, or assumed to be so; the ground-work for trust has Not been laid, the foundation has Not been poured or set and most assuredly there will Not be an activation of mutual trust! Despite hoping, thinking, and casually talking about the subject—no specified agreement = no engagement of trust. Contrary to popular opinion, great sex, marriage certificate, business partnerships, common interests, intellectually-stimulating conversations *do not naturally lead to an environment of mutually agreed trust. Like any other agreement, the engagement of trust must be thoroughly discussed, accepted, and agreed to by all involved.*

This can sometimes be challenging for some women to thoroughly and honestly participate in, esp. in our intimate relationships. Generally because of social conditioning, family of origin beliefs, birth order, religious constraints and other social norms. Women often *hope for*, what has never been fully discussed, clarified or agreed to by all. We do not want to appear pushy, too-masculine, or even worse—the b-word. We unwittingly, allow things "to slide" or be deferred for a "better time" or the "right time." When things do not work out as *hoped.* We are devastated, hurt, crushed, broken-hearted, embarrassed, humiliated, angry, depressed, shut-down. We *presumed* there was automatic trust in the relationship, business, or encounter because of the intensity, quality, outcome of the mutual activities. *Despite hoping, thinking, and casually talking about the subject—no specified agreement = no engagement of trust.*

When we see clearer, we know better…When we know better…it is incumbent on us…to do better…When we do not…we suffer.

K. Mhina Entrantt

The Ancient Rituals of Loving

The Ancients had a way of life where they knew how to integrate the many seasons of life together in an honorable way. Everyone spoke the same essence of *Language*. They had the same spiritual concepts, lines of integrity, principles, standards and ways of resolving disputes. In many aspects of life, we have lost our *Language* with one another; this is especially true, when it comes to the uniting of a man and a woman. There is no council, advisors, or guides to show and support an individual through the transformation from single adult to unified relationship with another. Who does an individual talk to in modern society that will give sound wisdom about this phase of life? Yes, there are those in various group associations that say they have the authority and knowledge to counsel dating couples, yet often their own relationship is in need of repair and falling apart.

For that reason, *the union of man and woman* has been reduced to simply finding sexual pleasure and financial security. The *true essence of a union* has been buried with the remains of our ancestors. Let us journey back and see how the Ancient Ones built relationship empires from the inside out. Let us become students again and learn of their ways and manners and see how they formed their unions of a man and a woman. Let us walk down the path of ancient times that we may retrieve what we have lost...

The Betrothed Period

The Betrothed Period was an Ancient Rite of the Egyptians, which was celebrated and adhered to for thousands of years. The Betrothed was a *Sacred Time for a couple*. For, *it was the time, when the couple agreed, to take the relationship to an advanced level, to determine their ability to be joined in a lifetime union.* It was very different from dating because now the couple was looking at their ability to form a spiritually sound, healthy, joyful life together. They had reached a point in their relationship where it seemed the other met the *initial* standards for forming a bond together. The Betrothed Period gave the couple the time to take a closer look at the person to see if they fit the other's life plans. After the great conquests, the Jews, Romans,

Greeks, and Celts claimed these rituals as their own and never gave rightful credit to its origin from the Egyptians.

A Betrothal is a Spiritually and Legally binding Agreement between a man and woman who share the same spiritual principles, complimentary life plans, mental soundness, and perspectives of life, to be joined in a lifetime union together.

The Ancient Egyptians established The Betrothed as the *time and season* when the *man encourages the woman to understand and accept him.* He does this through honest conversations about his strengths and challenges, successes and defeats, capacity to love and forgive, his immediate and long term life plans. *He allows the woman to know how she fits in his life and plans. He shows the woman daily by his actions and his words that he is a good choice for her.* He impresses her by how he conducts his affairs and how he deals with her on a daily basis. It is important to him to show her that he is the man for her; he is stable, kind, dependable, and reasonable. He does not take the Betrothed Period lightly.

The woman speaks candidly about the life she wishes to have for her and their offspring. She expresses how she sees her life in the present and the future. She makes it clear what her non-negotiables are regarding their life together. She is transparent with the man and allows him to know what her picture of life looks like and how she sees herself committing to those goals. She is not coy, indecisive, or expecting the man to know what she wants, without her speaking up. She does not agree to things, for which she knows she has no intention of doing or that she thinks she will eventually be able to convince him differently about. She is straight-forward in her discussions and gives her betrothed the opportunity to consider if what she desires and how she sees life is in *alignment* with his desires and how he sees his life and his future with her.

The woman allows for extended time to observe the man in all types of circumstances, to *determine, if the man is sound in his judgment and reasoning abilities, whether his life plans suit hers? Does he have character and integrity? Does his spirituality have deep roots? Mood? What is his reputation in his community? Can she see a life with this man that is in alignment with her desires and goals?* She frequently talks with him to see if her conclusions of him are accurate. She voices her joys and her concerns about her observations and she allows the man to discuss the matter from his perspective. *They honor and respect one another by asking; both the easy and the difficult questions; they leave nothing to chance or guessing what the other, wants/intended.* They learn to enjoy each other's company from a deeper more mature view, as they talk about their future life together.

At the end of the Betrothal Period both the man and woman are well informed about one another and whether the union meets the standards and requirements to be successful, according to each of their life plans and goals.

The couple has spent time together talking in great detail about their future life together. Each had at least a year or more to observe the other in a variety of circumstances. They were able to see how the other dealt with disappointment, conflict, family issues, finances, personality quirks, relaxation and fun.

Betrothed Rings:

Customs for Betrothed rings was also an Egyptian ritual. The Egyptian physicians taught that the fourth finger on the right hand is the vein that leads directly to the heart. It became known as "*the vein of love.*" Betrothed rings were always worn on the fourth finger. The Romans modified the Egyptian ring ceremony by placing the ring on the middle finger. The Romans often used the symbol of clasped hands on the betrothed rings to *symbolize a contract* between the man and the woman. The Irish modified the Roman customs by putting 2 hands clasping a heart on their betrothed rings.

In All of the animal kingdom there are mating rituals for each species. Some male birds go through elaborate dances, making nests, getting special berries to attract a mate. Female polar bears incite the males to run up and down snow embankments to prove his agility, physicality, and capability of producing healthy offspring. Flamingoes strut their stuff on the water and go through elaborate movements in order to choose a mate. Sea horses do a dance that lasts for hours as though it was choreographed to classical musical, as part of their mating ritual. The animal kingdom knows how to engage and have relationship with one another by nature and instinct. We would be wise to learn from them…

We have become like abandoned children, in our *Loving Relationship Patterns. We* vacillate between giving too much energy and emotional commitment too soon Or stop-and-go-initiations which always end in frustration and hurt feelings for all. We fear what we want, yet we keep trying to obtain. Our Unresolved hurts and traumas of the past, have full reign to determine how present and available we are in our present-day-relationships. We expect others to guess what we desire, without having dialogue and we throw tantrums when they get it wrong and we conclude they don't love us; when we never truly were available or open for Love. We identify great sex, shapely body parts, the size of the house, car, and bank account as the definition of Love. *We sabotage ourselves by repeating patterns which have never worked and then we curse Love and say it doesn't work!* We ask for what we are incapable of giving, from people who are incapable of receiving or giving. We ignore what we should confront and we confront what we have no control over. WE ARE OUT OF ALIGNMENT WITH OURSELVES AND OTHERS.

It is time to return to the Mother Principle…return to the guidance of our ancestors that we may again, be in alignment and balance with our union of man and woman. To continue on with the same lackluster is to destine ourselves to less than what the divine has to show us. It is not the *Fault of Men*… neither… the *Fault of Women; we have All lost our way and no longer know how to honor, engage, respect, be patient with, and love one another. We are confused, lost, angry, sad, hurt, and mis-informed children, pretending to know what we do not. It is time to Go Home and Be Taught…that we may Re-member who we truly are…and only then can we… Build Unions Again~*

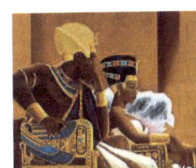

The Antiquity of Love

Oh My Black King let me love you down in the ways of the Ancient Ones.

Those who were once called, coppertones, kissed by the sun—the automatons, the great ones.

May we always remember our teachings and not succumb to the ways of the bump and grind and then we're done.

Oh My King, Let us Sing the Myths & Ancient songs from the Motherland;

the ones, that keep us focus, united, and strong.

Let our Love flow freely between us, to the Depths of the Seeds of Creativity,

that we, both came from.

Let us agree to love one another back-- from what all has been done.

Allow me to sit before you on bended knees, while holding your feet upon my lap.

And help you into your journey of bringing the real you back.

Let me hold your Worn feet between my soft healing hands;

Let my Smooth, Soothing touch tell you that I see a Strong Black Man!

As I Soak these feet in the Balm of Gilead & oils of Frankincense/Myrrh/Cinnabar;

The sweet fragrances Permeate the atmosphere, honoring Us for getting thus far.

I rub these feet in the warmest of waters,

I sense your body/mind/spirit as they begin to relax;

You and I—We Are Home....

Soak up the Strength My King- from the Nile, for as long as you like.

This is part of our home coming ritual-no need to be armed/fright.

As I bathe these feet I honor them with gratitude for carrying you to & fro.

For sustaining the load, even when all the doors seemed closed;

and every answer was "NO!"

I wash away the disappointment/frustration/sense of despair;

That came with the complexity of your day.

I sponge away, over & over the residue of fears of the unknown.

Encouraging you, to look toward your connection to the divine.

You smile, as you remember the Great Mother and how she's always there;

Just waiting for your call and to show you how much she cares.

I, your Queen rejoice with you as I and we are embraced by the Mother,

It is never what it may seem. We must always expect the miracle, the vision, the dream.

I point to the stars and we both smile as we remember who we really are.

I lull you to sleep in the knowing that you have come home again--

Home to the Ancient Ones...Again!

I whisper in your ear…as you drift off to sleep…

Oh My King, we have made it back Home again…

Our Union is complete…

You pull me in closer and deeper into your arms

and you whisper in my ear…

Welcome Home My Queen~

The Flight of the Crows

As the New Breed Crows allowed themselves to be

separated/divided/assimilated by the deception of the Dove Nation;

Un-beknownst to them,

was a Secret-Society of Crows Underground (S.S.C.U.s)

S.S.C.U.s were started by the Ancient Crows who saw

The Dove the first day he came to their tree,

Olive branch in mouth, pretending 2 bring peace.

In the middle of the night the young baby crows

Were rousted, awakened by the Ancient Ones/Scrybes/Elders

To be taught their true heritage and the meaning

Of each plume and where it came from.

There were special Dawn Days, when Crow Mother Matriarche Crow

Would show up herself, 2 teach the Baby Crows about their rich heritage and wealth.

She taught them lullabyes to sing about the galaxies/ moon/stars.

She reminded them even when they didn't see her, she wasn't far.

She divided the Baby Crows into groups of 3.

Each group had a secret code, but not all 3.

This was her way of protecting Black Crow Mysteries.

So even if one was captured and beaten until he/she revealed

their code, not even that crow would know where the rest abode.

When the Crow Scribes were not teaching the Baby Crows;

They were writing on the walls underground.

They knew the teachings & principles would be safe,

where it could not be found.

No one would look there, because everybody knows

Crows don't go underground.

The Baby Crows were fed special foods and nectar from above.

That when they stood before the Doves, their food or drink

They would never crave or love.

From these Baby Crows came the Greater Crow Nation (G.C.N.)

As the tainted crows, died out; by their own, assimilation and infiltration of Dove-Mis-education.

The Greater Crown Nation continues to thrive, unto this day.

Right before the confused Doves' eyes.

As they scratch their trickery heads

And wonder how and why, given their tactics—

All the crows didn't die.

K. Mhina Entrantt © 2011

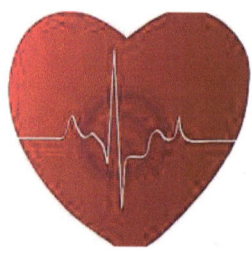

Except You and I...

Except the One Living the life,

makes a decision to continue on,

to grow, to learn, to forgive oneself

and others, to laugh and live out loud!

No one can save them from their choice

to die, while still standing.

Except the broken-heart be mended, healed

The depth and sincerity of the New Love

that shows up,

will not matter,

for the heart will not

have regained its ability to hear and feel--again.

Except Truth be pursued with the diligence of a foot-soldier,

Mistakes/Lies/Rumors/Gossip will always

find a taker to spread them further.

Except Peace & Harmony dwell in the same house,

the architect/the builder/all the carpenters

have but wasted their time and energy,

for the house will never be able to stand.

Except the 5%ers and the 10%ers find common ground

and learn how to create a dual common language,

the 1%ers will always be pulling the un-suspecting strings

of the 99%.

Except I See & Acknowledge the Divinity in You

And You See & Acknowledge in Me;

we are doomed to be perpetual enemies and strangers.

Except you go forward in your Vision and

Create what has Never been seen/done,

your life will remain Incomplete

And so will Ours~

K. Mhina Entrantt© 2011

Part III: Coming Home

The Crane Girl

A girl by the name of Shazaer from the town of Intrigue and New Journeys was sent to find a crane and bring back proof she had met the Cranes.

She was well fortified for her journey with the right clothing, snacks and water, for it was her grandmother who had sent her on this journey. Grandmother promised Shazaer that she would receive a wonderful gift if she could meet the cranes.

The first day of her journey Shazaer sang and danced on the path, stopping along the way to make sure she had not missed the movement of the cranes. She saw some of the most beautiful birds, many she had not seen before, but no cranes were in sight.

Shazaer held on to Grandmother's promise of a great gift, if she met the cranes. Just the thought of this made her very happy. So she journeyed on… Three days had passed before Shazaer lay down to rest on a soft spot in between 2 look-a-like-trees. It was such a comfortable spot she drifted off to sleep. As Shazaer slept the Cranes came.

Mrs. Crane hovered over Shazaer to try to make heads or tales, of what she was seeing—a very brown girl with rows of braids hanging on her shoulder, a sack of human food with a toy at the bottom and a wooden container of water. Before she could stop them, the youngest crane children—the twins had pecked holes in the wood and were drinking the water.

Mrs. Crane scolded the boys, but it was too late they had drank all the water, while Shazaer soundly slept. The boys felt bad and replaced the water and sealed the holes with hardened mud. It was just as they had finished sealing the last hole and flew away that Shazaer awoke. She noticed the ground beside her was damp and thought that was odd, for her wooden water container was full. She thought to herself, she didn't realize she had put so much water in it. She shrugged her shoulders and continued to go North, as she had been instructed by Grandmother.

When Mr. Crane came home, Mrs. Crane and the twins told him all about their day with the tall brown-face girl with the braids. "Hmmmm said Mr. Crane, I will tell the others to keep a look out. I wonder, what brings her here? I'm glad she stopped at the Sleeping Willow Trees."

Hidden from the cranes were the BAD Bird Crew (BADs), listening to every word. "We gotta do something about this girl said Broadwaysz the teenager. I'm tired of the humans always coming to our land uninvited! Let's get some rocks and sticks so we can beat her, that will teach the humans what happens when they trespass on our land! We all know how peaceful the cranes are, they'd give her a gift and tell her to come back anytime! I'm not having it—NOT THIS TIME!" The other BADs chanted with Broadwaysz—"Not this time!" "Not this time!" "Not this time!"

As Jarard sat down beside the marsh to look around he could hear the BADs shouting and fussing about something. He decided to hide behind the grass to see what they were up to. Whatever it was, it wasn't going to be good. Jarard and his family were the only humans that had ever been allowed to live here. His grandparents had helped the King and Queen fight against a strong enemy that was trying to conquer the kingdom, When the war was over, the King and Queen decreed Jarard's family would always have land, abundance, and a castle to live in until the 10th generation. The oath had the King and Queen's ring signet on it and it was read before the entire kingdom. The BADs didn't like it but they knew not to go against the King and Queen, who ruled in love, harmony, and peace.

Shazaer traveled 3 more days, still no sign of the cranes. Every so often she would feel a rock pass her and a few actually hit her, but there was nobody there. Maybe it was the wind, moving the rocks around, there was a light breeze. Shazaer took off her shoes for her feet were hurting and she put them in the cool water. The BADs saw this as their chance to teach the human-girl a lesson. They came charging at Shazaer and she fell into the lake as the BADs taunted her. Shazaer was not a very good swimmer and she began to cry and scream for help. Everyone in the kingdom heard it and was alarmed for they had never heard a cry of fear before. The Cranes were the first to arrive at the lake. The other birds quickly fastened leaves together to pull the human-girl out the lake and dry her off. In all the commotion, the BADs were backing away from the crowd, when Mr. Crane said "not so fast, what did you do to the human girl that made her bring fear to our Kingdom?!" Everybody looked at Broadwaysz who began to stutter saying—"Well-we-ll. W-e-ll, she had no business coming here the humans have taken over and have destroyed almost everything—all around us! I wasn't going to let her do that to our Kingdom. Somebody had to teach her a lesson!" Everyone shook their heads in disbelief as the BADs hid in the grass beside Jarard.

Shazaer sat shivering with the leaf blanket around her, still crying about being afraid in the water. She stopped crying when she realized she was surrounded by cranes, other beautiful birds, animals, and trees. They were all talking about her, looking at her. She could not believe her eyes or her ears! Mrs. Crane flew to her side and asked her "why have you come all this way to our land dear?" Shazaer was so startled she began to have the hiccups and tried to speak in between the hiccups. "M-y G-G-Grandmother sss-ent meee to find the cranes and give you a gift." She reached in her wet bag and pulled out a miniature plaque which had a carving of a crane on it and the words Thank You. All the other crane families came closer to get a better look at the plaque. It was beautiful and full of colors like the feathers of the cranes. All the others were astonished at the beauty of the plaque and wondered what it meant. Even the BADs were intrigued.

About that time the Elder Cranes made their way through the crowd and begin to speak in *the Ancient Tongue*. They took the plaque up to the tallest tree and begin to sing and dance. Everyone in the Kingdom began to fall to their knees, for they knew something *Sacred* was happening for the Elders to speak in the Ancient Tongue. The Elders flew in swooping patterns, sang and danced for an hour. Nobody moved until the Matriarche said, "*All Rise!*"

With tears streaming down his face Grandfather Crane began to tell the story of a great loss that happened in their Kingdom many generations ago. Some of the eggs of their tribe had been stolen by the humans. Because the eggs were so young, when the humans got them, within the shell the baby cranes begin to turn into humans instead of cranes, except a few. Three nursemaids were also stolen from the Crane Tribe to take care of the children. It was the nursemaids who secretly taught the children the Old Way. The plaque was secretly given to one of the nursemaids to give to the child who would make it back to the tribe. That is when everyone turned back to look at Shazaer...

As Grandfather Crane was finishing up his last words, something begin to happen to Shazaer, she metamorphosed into a Crane and began to fly. The entire Crane Nation joined her in flight and they celebrated with a V formation, while those on the ground sang, danced, and clapped their hands. The King and Queen declared it an official wholly-day and the Kingdom celebrated for weeks, that the stolen egg had made her way back home.

K. Mhina Entrantt©2013

An Allegory/Apologue

An allegory presents a way of looking at a situation to gain understanding, enlightenment, and a desire to address or change what has been one's past response. It is shown through artistic expressions such as a story, play, poem, etc. The main purpose of an allegory is to get one's attention on a specific matter. The allegory gives insight that provokes one to take the necessary actions for a better life.

During the Ancient Days, many of the tribes, kin, and elders of the nations of Egyptians, Chinese, Native Americans, Japanese, East Indians, South Americans and many others revered the lessons of the plant and animal kingdoms and passed these lessons down to the next generation through oral traditions and celebrations. The animal kingdom and the plant kingdom have always been available to give us so much more than the sustenance of food. We have often missed or overlooked these lessons of life, for we thought we were above the other forms of life.

Since the beginning of time, nature has tried her best to teach us about the insidious principles of life. The Cranes were considered sacred birds, referred to as messengers of god. Many looked to the behavior of the cranes to predict when a storm was approaching. In ancient ceremonies the Cranes were honored for showing the people how to go with the flow of life and to reach for higher levels of spirituality. As the sun's journey impacts all living things, we as humans must yield to the natural flow and order as nature does.

During the various conquests of history the Romans and Greeks engrafted many of these traditions and symbols too. There was a time when the crane was a common bird in Britain and Ireland. It was associated with the Scottish goddess Cailleach and the Irish god Manannan mac Lir.

Creating your own Allegory for Coming Home...

Once upon a time called the Ancient Days of Today there lived a_____(girl, boy, woman, man, animal, bird, or plant) who....

Close your eyes, take 3 deep inhaling, exhaling breaths, count from 1,030 down to 1,000. Open your eyes, start writing to add to the above sentence. Write for 5 minutes or more. You can write on paper or use a computer. Do not get distracted by misspelled words or punctuations. Just write until you feel you are complete.

The Desire to come Home was so strong that I...

Close your eyes, take 3 deep inhaling, exhaling breaths, count from 1,030 down to 1,000. Open your eyes, start writing to add to the above sentence. Write for 12 minutes or more. You can write on paper or use a computer.

Everywhere I went people were talking about coming home. I heard songs about coming home on the radio. I saw movies about coming home, but I wasn't ready. I didn't know how to come home, so
I_____
_____
_____
_____

Instead of coming home.

Close your eyes, take 3 deep inhaling, exhaling breaths, count from 1,030 down to 1,000. Open your eyes, start writing to add to the above sentence. Write for 10 minutes or more. You can write on paper or use a computer.

I resisted coming home Until...

Close your eyes, take 3 deep inhaling, exhaling breaths, count from 1,030 down to 1,000. Open your eyes, start writing to add to the above sentence. Write for 5 minutes or more. You can write on paper or use a computer.

 After I made the Decision to come home I....

Write until you are complete.

Epilogue

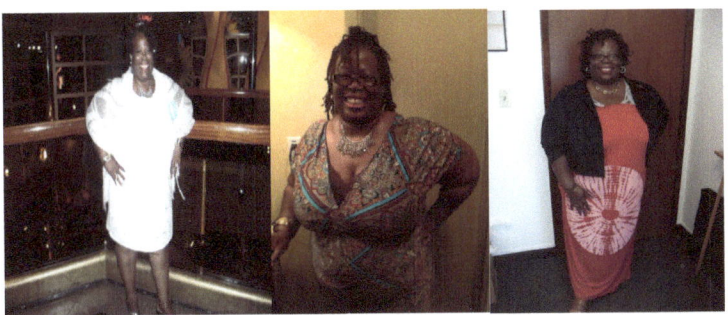

I Am an Empress of Enlightenment, Webster's New Dictionary describes enlightenment, as to inform, to free from lack of knowledge, unawareness, or experience. I have accepted my sacred contract to unfold to others the simplicity of the Law of Attraction. I walk in the practical Principles of Tjeuti, what the world often refers to as the Hermetic or Thoth Principles, the 7 natural laws which govern the universe. The Law of Attraction is not a get-rich-quick scheme or an abbra-cadabra-of-getting-what-you-want by the snap of a finger. The Law of Attraction is a universal law, which the ancients honored and adhered to for thousands of years. It is as real as the Law of Gravity; everyone accepts if you jump off a tall building without supporting ropes, you will come crashing down to the ground. Everyone accepts and expects the light to come on when you flip the switch.

No one thinks about the universal governing laws which make electricity a reality. The frequency of the radio waves and what that truly means… is not even a fleeting thought in our everyday world. As well, the energy for heating, air conditioning and cooking on a stove, slip by most of our conscious minds. That does not change the reality of the governing laws and how they work seamlessly. Embracing the Law of Attraction allows us to work in union and harmony with the universal laws, instead of in opposition and out of synch.

> *There is One Ultimate Reality, but within this One are many experiences. Man is within the One and draws from it all his experiences. As man thinks he subjectifies thought and sets in motion, through the Medium of the Universal Mind. This Law works automatically until it is consciously changed. To learn how to think is to learn how to live, for our thoughts go into a Medium that is infinite in its ability to be and to do. Man is using a power which is infinite, as compared with the power of his conscious thought.*
>
> The Science of Mind, Earnest Holmes

The Law of Attraction is a practice and a discipline, similar to prayer, meditation, yoga, and fasting. In its truest form it is not so much about getting everything checked off of your wants and desires lists; it is about acquiring a state of awareness that reminds you of the power of your thoughts. Thoughts truly are things, little and not so little entities, which show up in your physical world. The more you think about what you do not want and how awful things are…the more it will continue to show up, despite the fact that you do not want to have these awful things in your life. It is an Absolute that, what you focus on with animated emotion will show up in your life, emotions, and body. There is no getting around this ancient axiom. Most people go through life, without having this awareness or without understanding *how* the Law of Attraction works or lack acceptance that this applies to their life situations.

> *There is nothing in the universal order that denies the individual's good, or self-expression, so long as such self-expression does not contradict the general good, does not contradict Goodness itself. There is nothing in the Universe that denies us the right to be happy, if our happiness does not deny, interfere with the general good. The Universe remains unlimited, though the world has suffered a sense of limitation. We should be careful not to divide our mental house against itself.*
>
> *Our beliefs, and our deep-seated convictions inevitably out-picture and reflect themselves in our experience and environment, both in the physical condition of the body and in the larger world of our affairs. What we outwardly are, and what we are to become, depends upon our thinking, for this is the way we are using Creative Power.*
>
> The Science of Mind, Earnest Holmes

The Law of Attraction is about Coming Home within your own body/mind/ spirit— it is the next natural step as 4th Chakrah experiences of opening and healing the heart, give way to the in-coming 5th and 6th Chakrahs. This is the return of the child-like passion for life, for now you recognize yourself; no longer taunted/haunted/identified by the descriptions of others. The physical body begins to repair, rejuvenate, and call back the breath of life unto you. The mind begins to let go of the continuous searches for all the *little whys* of how previous circumstances have gone, upon doing this, a higher level of Forgiveness for self and others opens up, effortlessly. As Forgiveness settles in; depressions, unresolved anger, and feelings of unworthiness begin to fall away. The spirit within begins to soar, expand, and express the fullness of divine essence. These are the gifts of The Law of Attraction, available to all who will respond to the call~

> *The power of the Lord was upon me and I was carried away by the Spirit of the Lord to a valley full of old, dry bones that were scattered everywhere across the ground. He led me around among them and then he said to me: Son of dust can these bones become people again? I replied, "Lord you alone know the answer to that." Then he told me to speak to the bones and say: O dry bones listen to the words of God, for the Lord says See! I am going to make you live and breathe again! I will replace the flesh and muscles on you and cover you with skin. I will put breath into you and you shall live and know I am the Lord. So I spoke these words from God just as he told me to: and suddenly there was a rattling noise from all across the valley, and the bones of each body came together and attached to each other as they used to be. Then as I watched, the muscles and flesh formed over the bones, and skin covered them, but the bones had no breath. Then he told me to call to the wind and say: The Lord God says: Come from the four winds, O spirit and breathe upon these slain bodies, that they may live again." So I spoke to the wind as he commanded me and the bodies began breathing: they lived and stood up—a very great army.*

Ezekiel 37: 1-10, Living Bible

I Care About You!

In this maze of days, we call life,

Seemingly, mixed with sadness & strife.

And even for those that most things go right,

There are still daysz when they feel a little uncertain;

and deal with bouts of fright.

For you, me and All of us

I write this scribe, that on downward days,

You have some words of nourishment, upon which

You can rely:

I Care about u and all the craziness

that you've been through.

I Care about the way your crooked- twists & turns .

I Care about how you laid awake at night, wondering

If anybody was concerned—about you…

I Care about how the relationship ended w/

the one you thought would be ur boo,

forever true.

I Care about the tears you cried &

the pit in the bottom of ur stomach

that kept getting tighter & tighter

after you found ur gurle w/ ur boi.

I know u told urself man-up

but I understand that kinda

hurt & betrayal is tuff!

I Care that sometimes you feel like

the harder u try, the deeper the hole get and-

the smaller ur paycheck gets-and-the higher the

bills get & sometimes u juss want to quit!

I Care about how hard it is to raise a

Man-Childe, when his daddy ain't around

or daddy is a childe too.

I Care about how challenging it is to see daddy's little gurle,

That you raised on your own, now, giving you lip and thinking she's Grown.

I Care about all those fears you have about

Baby Gurle, as she's sliding into lil-womanhood.

You try to prepare her, but ur not sure if ur

words w/ her are doin any good...

I Care about how you compare urself to what media

says is pretty/acceptable/sexy/desirable/perfect

and u disown the parts of u that will never

 measure up

to the air-brushed-stuff!

I Care that what the ads call a man, you know will Never

Help a man be who he was meant to be; shaking hands and being in alignment with his true ?Destiny.

I Care about u, the innocent one whose most

preciousness was taken by someone u trusted,

now their acts play w/ ur head, have u thinking

u're the disgusted one.

I Care about u drowning ur sorrows & disappointments

in a 5th of this & a bottle of that...or...a pipe...a track...

I Care about u, 3 strikes gone

never to return to the community or ur home.

I Care about u w/ a sentence of 100+ years,

having to instantly say goodbye to everything

u hold as dear;

in order to condition urself

 for another atmosphere...

I Care about the children trying to sort out things

far beyond their development years, most of it

emotional debris from grown-folksz fears...

I Care about u when u're up.

I Care about u when u're down.

I Care about u when u got it right,

I Care about u when

u went about it/at it oh so wrong...

I Care about u when u fall on ur own mistakes.

I Care about u when u realize it's still not 2 late.

I Care about u when u're hungry.

I Care about u when u're full.

I Care about u when u're lonely.

I Care about u when u're surrounded by love.

I Care about u when u're angry, even if it's w/ me.

I Care about u when u're calm & peaceful.

I Care about u when u're confused/distorted/dark...

I Care about u when u're in at-one-ment/harmony/light...

Oh My People How I Care about you~

© 2010 K. Mhina Entrantt

Dr. K. Mhina Entrantt, Winter 2013

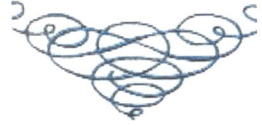

K. Mhina Entrantt Products and Materials

I Found My Voice can be found on Amazon and lulu.com. All other books can be found on www.lulu.com. All of these materials can also be found locally at:

L.E.M.S. Book Store 5023 Rainier Avenue S. Seattle WA 98118 206 650-8791

ECO-ELEMENTS 1530 First Avenue Seattle, WA 98101 206 467-7745

Poetry:

www.gspoetry.com (MHina)

Videos

www.Vimeo.com/Karen Entrantt

Baby Girle

Can Love Bring her Back!

When a Woman Respects her Man

2 Artists 1 Love

A Love Conversation

The Family Table

Work it out and Stay!

What is Success?

Articles

http://www.allthingshealing.com/Poetry-Therapy/Poetry-is-MY-Therapy-Healing-Power-of-Your-Paper-Pen/8870#.Tkv_KeSSP-4.email

www.napturalroots.com/Karen Entrantt

Dr. K. Mhina Entrantt, Ph.D, is a Life Coach, Poet, Motivational Speaker, and Author of 5 books. Dr. K has worked in the fields of Social Work, Mental Health Professional, Homelessness Prevention, and Women Services for over 33 years. Dr. K has spent her career helping others reach their potential and individual successes.

Dr. K is passionate about helping others overcome obstacles and reach their personal goals. To have her as a Life Coach or to attend one of her workshops is "an unforgettable, fantastic, life-changing experience!" As, many participants, state on their evaluation sheets. She uses her own real-world terms, strategies, humor, and interactive participation to help those she coaches and attendees become eager to embrace the next level of their own life expansion.

Dr. K is willing to be your Life Coach or bring these workshops to your meetings, gatherings, agency trainings, conferences, conventions, church and civic functions

Dr. K is also a story-teller and performing-poet. She has performed at The Act Theater, Seattle Town Hall, Westlake Mall and many other public and private venues. Dr. K is also available to perform her life changing poetry at any event. Workshops can also be tailored to fit your specific group needs. K_poetry_seminars@yahoo.com

www.ingramcontent.com/pod-product-compliance
Lightning Source LLC
Chambersburg PA
CBHW041351290426
44108CB00001B/13